ENGLISH GRAIN EXPORTS
AND
THE STRUCTURE OF AGRARIAN CAPITALISM
1700–1760

Hull University Press

Occasional Papers in Economic and Social History
No. 12

General Editor: John Saville
*Emeritus Professor of Economic and Social History
in the University of Hull*

ENGLISH GRAIN EXPORTS AND THE STRUCTURE OF AGRARIAN CAPITALISM 1700–1760

DAVID ORMROD

Lecturer in Economic and Social History
University of Kent

HULL UNIVERSITY PRESS
1985

© David Ormrod 1985
ISBN 0 85958 445 3
ISSN 0078 3013

Phototypeset in 11 on 12 pt Baskerville
Book Ens, Saffron Walden, Essex
Printed and bound in Great Britain

For my parents

'It is one question, how to treat your fields so as to get a good harvest; another whether you wish to have a good harvest or would rather like to keep up the price of corn.'

John Ruskin, *A Joy for ever: and its price in the market* (1857; rev. ed. 1897) p. 43.

'He that withholdeth corn, the people shall curse him: but blessing shall be upon the head of him that selleth it.'

Proverbs xi: 26

CONTENTS

List of Tables and Figures

Abbreviations

AAG Bijdragen	*Afdeling Agrarische Geschiedenis Bijdragen*
Annales ESC	*Annales (Economies, Sociétés, Civilisations)*
BL Add. Mss.	British Library, Additional Manuscripts
BPP	British Parliamentary Papers
Econ. Hist. Rev.	*Economic History Review*
GAA	Gemeente Archief, Amsterdam
GAR	Gemeente Archief, Rotterdam
HUL	Brynmor Jones Library, University of Hull
NRO	Northumberland Record Office
NNRO	Norfolk and Norwich Record Office
N. Arch.	Notarial Archives
PRO	Public Record Office

1 Primitive Accumulation and the Problem of Agrarian Capitalism

In both the immediate post-war and more recent discussions of the historical conditions for the transition from feudalism to capitalism, there has been an apparently inescapable tendency to strike a false polarity between those economic and social changes which are thought to originate in the sphere of production and those which are thought to centre on exchange and the market – what Eric Hobsbawm has described as a constant dialogue between the productionists and the marketeers, which at times breaks down into a monologue.[1] The traditional Marxist view which Maurice Dobb has usually been thought to represent was to emphasise the production side, a position which was especially strong in the 1930s when Soviet historians were encouraged to criticise the work of Pokrovsky who, it was felt, had over-emphasised the role of merchant capitalism in the transition process, and to construct a kind of productivism, resting upon the primacy of invention, scientific advance, technical change and the progress of handicrafts, in its place.[2] This false antithesis was expressed in the Dobb/Sweezy debate of the early 1950s and exaggerated in subsequent commentaries on that debate, and has been conspicuously revived by Robert Brenner who represents Wallerstein, Frank and Sweezy as subscribers to a 'Neo-Smithian Marxism' resting on the progressive role of the market.[3] Among non-Marxist economic historians too, there has certainly been a strong emphasis on the primacy of changes in international trade and commercial relations in English and European economic development, following, though not necessarily deriving from, Tawney's pioneering work on the genesis of commercial capitalism.[4]

The supposed contradiction between those explanations of capitalist origins which focus on production and those which focus

1

on trade and markets, between capitalist agriculture and merchant capitalism, is difficult to dislodge, because it is one which is deeply rooted in the history of economic thought. It is present in Marx's own writing, and it can be traced back to the different emphasis placed upon agriculture and trade in the thought of the Physiocrats, especially Quesnay, and that of Adam Smith.[5] For the Physiocrats, of course, wealth centred on land and agriculture; for Adam Smith, wealth was multiplied through division of labour which was limited only by the size of the market and restrictions on commerce. Smith's point of departure from the Physiocrats was in arguing for a trade-induced division of labour, involving an increased separation of economic activities as between town and countryside, and book three of the *Wealth of Nations* consists of a rarely-noticed historical description of three processes which he felt explained 'the progress of opulence in different nations', namely, 'the Discouragement of Agriculture in the ancient State of Europe, after the Fall of the Roman Empire'; 'the Rise and Progress of Cities and Towns after the Fall of the Roman Empire'; and 'How the Commerce of Towns contributed to the Improvement of the Country'.[6] It is important to recognise that Marx absorbed the ideas of both the Physiocrats and Adam Smith, and realised that in some important respects, Smith 'inherited the legacy of the Physiocrats';[7] indeed, J. P. Cooper explained how Turgot's ideas provide a link between those of Quesnay and Smith, through to Marx: 'Turgot generalized the notion of capitalism by clarifying Quesnay's conception of advances in agriculture and extending it to commerce and manufacturing' hence 'Marx's system belonged consciously to a well established tradition whose model was a unilinear evolution by stages towards a commercialized market-dominated economy'.[8] But these links are fragile, and in his historical exposition of the transition from feudalism to capitalism in England, Marx seems to have separated these two strands of thought without demonstrating historically how they came together. The ideas of the Physiocrats were examined in detail in *Theories of Surplus Value* (1862) and Smith's 'historical' chapters in the *Wealth of Nations* were utilised in the *Grundrisse* (1857/8).[9] The separation is most evident in *Capital* however, and hinges on the question of primitive accumulation,

Marx's answer to the problem of the origin of capital in pre-capitalist societies. Marx gave two different answers to this question. The first, elaborated in volume one, is agrarian, productionist, and rooted in the class structure of rural society. It was the creation of a rural proletariat through the expropriation of the peasantry, which 'received a new and frightful impulse from the Reformation, and from the consequent colossal spoilation of Church property.'[10] The primitive accumulation of volume one is therefore 'nothing more than the historical process of divorcing the producer from the means of production'.[11] But this process presupposes the existence of capital, and in volume three, an alternative answer is given in terms of money, markets and exchange, that is, the rise of merchant's capital and its adjunct, usurer's capital. Merchant's capital was described by Marx as 'older than the capitalist mode of production', and 'since merchant's capital is penned in the sphere of circulation, and since its function consists exclusively of promoting the exchange of commodities, it requires no other conditions for its existence – aside from the undeveloped forms arising from direct barter – outside those necessary for the simple circulation of commodities and money.'[12] Merchant's capital and commodity circulation is therefore seen as an early source of capital within the feudal mode of production and a real basis for primitive accumulation.

How are these two strands in the history of capitalism to be connected, and is their 'separation' merely a textual illusion? To answer these questions, it is necessary to clear away some misunderstanding of the contribution made by earlier commentators, especially Tawney and Dobb, after recapitulating what might be described as the consensus of recent historiography; and it is also worth considering the historical circumstances which generated the initial interest of the eighteenth-century political economists in the question of primitive accumulation, whose ideas were central to Marx's understanding of the problem.

At the outset, it is clear that Marx overestimated the extent of peasant dispossession in the sixteenth century. We need not necessarily share Althusser's fear of a 'debilitating Hegelian influence' in volume one of *Capital* in order to accept Hindess and Hirst's claim that the chief value of the historical chapters of volume one lies in their polemical quality rather than in providing a scientific understanding of the transition from feudalism to capitalism.[13] The arguments and historical material of volume three, in relation to merchant's capital, are more rigorous and well-authenticated if less well known, and do not merely rest on the transforming effects of overseas trade and an expanding world market. In his anxiety to reject a 'commercialisation model' of capitalist origins, however, Brenner has revived the analysis of volume one and restates how the disposal of customary peasant tenures in the sixteenth century provided the basis for agrarian capitalism – what one commentator has described as 'political marxism'. 'As the role of the class struggle is widely under-estimated, so he [Brenner] injects strong doses of it into historical explanation' amounting to 'a volontarist vision of history in which the class struggle is divorced from all other objective contingencies',[14] especially the mode of production itself. The peasantry is thus eliminated from participating in agricultural development except in terms of its disappearance. Yet much recent research has shown how small proprietors provided the backbone of agrarian improvement especially by promoting new crops and their diffusion. Summarising work by Cornwall, Havinden, Thirsk and others, Croot and Parker conclude that Brenner has greatly inflated the role of the large 'capitalist' farmer and the large farm in the sixteenth and early seventeenth centuries and suggest that 'The peasant, far from being an obstacle to economic development, may actually have supplied its impetus by adopting new practices or new crops or just by showing landlords the profits that good husbandry could bring.'[15] Both Marxist and non-Marxist historians have described how the disappearance of the peasantry was a slow process spread over the three centuries from 1500 to 1800, becoming especially intense during the late seventeenth and early eighteenth centuries; and that this was less a case of forcible expropriation than one involving transfer of the surplus through the intensification of market relations – increases in rents and fines, and peasant land sales.[16] The course of public opinion and legislation, and the history of pamphlet literature and popular disturbance reveals a Tudor agrarian problem which was real enough and which centred

4

on the difficulty of finding pasture for a growing population at a time when most farmers wanted to increase the scale of their operations, particularly in the 1540s and the early seventeenth century.[17] But, as Joan Thirsk argues, complaints against enclosure and engrossing lost some of their sting in the second half of the sixteenth century and the movement probably slowed down; moreover, 'the idea that enclosure had some merit was gaining ground, as reasonable methods of carrying it through became more common and the peasantry shared in its benefits.'[18]

The effect of Brenner's attempt to reconstruct an exaggerated class struggle/expropriation view of sixteenth-century agrarian changes has been to sharpen the separation between agrarian and merchant capitalism, and between the arguments of Dobb and Sweezy – those of the former being shown in a severely productionist light.[19] Dobb in fact, like Tawney writing before him, recognised that the sixteenth century was characterised by a specifically *commercial* form of capitalism and drew on the insights of both Tawney and Unwin to elaborate this. The agrarian capitalism discussed by Tawney in *The Agrarian Problem* was identified with the commercialisation of agriculture. The agrarian changes of the sixteenth century, Tawney suggested, 'may be regarded as a long step in the commercialisation of English life' with the growth of the textile industries and the woollen export trade seen as dependent on the development of pasture farming.[20] In a penetrating assessment of Tawney's *Agrarian Problem*, Dr Havinden has argued that its main assertion was not that customary tenants were evicted in large numbers (the caricature presented by some of Tawney's critics) but that they were obliged to pay higher entry fines; and that 'it was the commercialisation of agriculture, by which the profits were transferred to landlords rather than retained by peasants, which constituted the most revolutionary agrarian change in the sixteenth century.'[21] Indeed, the evidence for much of this transfer, in the shape of the sharply rising level of rents in the later sixteenth century, was provided by that most strident of Tawney's critics, Dr Kerridge.[22]

While Tawney did much to establish the extent of market penetration within sixteenth-century agriculture, Dobb, in the middle chapters of his *Studies*, went on to discuss the commercialisation of industry in the same period, relying heavily and extensively upon historical material from George Unwin's *Studies in Industrial Organisation in the Sixteenth and Seventeenth Centuries* to elaborate Marx's familiar suggestion that industrial capital developed in two main ways:[23]

> According to the first – 'the really revolutionary way' – a section of the producers themselves accumulated capital and took to trade, and in course of time began to organize production on a capitalist basis free from the handicraft restrictions of the gilds. According to the second, a section of the existing merchant class began to 'take possession directly of production'; thereby 'serving historically as a mode of transition', but becoming eventually 'an obstacle to a real capitalist mode of production and declin(ing) with the development of the latter'.

It is important to realise that while Dobb discussed the decline of feudalism in agrarian and clearly productionist terms, his analysis of the rise of capitalism rested squarely upon the transforming effects of merchant's capital. Trade and markets, he argued, had 'an important reciprocal influence on production' and were 'to be assigned a leading rôle at various points in the story'. Indeed, 'Trade was the soil from which a bourgoisie first grew.'[24] What Dobb actually argued against was the notion, propagated by Pokrovsky, of a special period of merchant capitalism, distinguished only by large-scale trading operations and the appearance of a merchant class, and any strictures against merchant capitalism, he held, should not apply to those who recognise the early period of capitalism when production was subordinated to the merchant manufacturer under the putting out system.[25] This defensiveness and reserve about merchant capitalism no doubt reflected the violent reaction against Pokrovsky's ideas and career amongst Soviet historians during the later 1930s, and not without good reason. Pokrovsky's main argument, propounded during the 1920s, was that the three and a half centuries from 1564 to 1917 in Russian history were distinguished by a system of commercial capitalism, with the October Revolution seen as the objective result of a long period of capitalist development: an analysis which both challenged the moderates' argument that Russia was not prepared for a socialist revolution in 1917 as well as that of the left opposition that rapid socialist development was limited by Russia's economic backwardness. When, during the first of Stalin's five year plans, this stress on the advanced character of the pre-revolutionary economy no longer seemed appropriate, Pokrovsky's pronouncements became increasingly inconsistent, and in 1931, he asserted that the period of merchant capitalism should be regarded more correctly as one of 'non-classical feudalism'.[26] Soon after his death in 1932, his work was officially discredited, and in his discussion of the activities of the Historians' Group of the British Communist Party, Hobsbawm singles out the 'complex discussions on "merchant capital" which accompanied the criticism of M. N. Pokrovsky' in the Soviet Union, as being well known to that group.[27] But by 1962, Dobb felt that it was reasonable to identify merchant capitalism as a precursor stage, an 'immature and undeveloped first stage of capitalism in England for two centuries before 1800', though definitely not as a separate system or mode of production.[28]

In terms of historical substance therefore, the transforming effects of merchant's capital within agriculture and industrial activity have never been seriously in doubt, although earlier writers may have been misunderstood or misrepresented. And it is clear that the connection between these two major strands in the history of capitalism, the circulation of merchant's capital and capitalist relations of production, lies in the process of *internal commercialisation*. The most succinct expression of this relationship is perhaps to be found in Medick's work which shows how the 'functional interrelationship between the [peasant] family economy and merchant capital' was worked out in terms of proto-industrialisation.[29] The historical literature relating to domestic production, especially of woollen textiles, is, of course, extensive and well known. The interconnections between domestic textile production and the wider commercial economy were outlined by Supple many years ago in his work on early seventeenth-century commercial crises'[30] and Nef's exaggerated claims for the role of centralised and capital-intensive industrial production in the early modern economy were criticised and abandoned even earlier.[31] Jones and Thirsk, among others, have drawn attention to the agricultural origins of industry in terms of the processing of farm products, and to the resilience and adaptability of the dual economy of the pastoral regions.[32] The slow emergence of capitalist industry as a residual element out of the multiplicity of by-employments and crafts practised by the peasant household has now become one of the well-established supports of early modern historiography. The novelty and value of Medick's work however, lies in linking the proto-industrial family economy to the history of the mode of production.

Medick's analysis, following Chayanov, rests on the inter-relationships and tension between an unstable macro-historical situation, the disintegration of traditional peasant society, and the stable micro-historical phenomenon of the self-regulating peasant household-economy. At the macro-level, we can speak of a transition during the early modern period from land intensive agrarian production to labour intensive craft production in rural areas, relying on the labour of an under-employed class of small peasants and landless labourers, increasingly penetrated by merchant capital both internally and on the world market.[33] There could be no clearer indication of the extent of that transition in England than the severity of the commercial crisis of the 1620s, which brought widespread distress to small producers.[34] At the micro-level, the household economy was characterised by self-exploitation by the family in the production of craft goods, and this enabled the merchant or putting-out capitalist to realise a 'differential profit', since the merchant subtracted from the price of labour what the family produced on its own landholding.[35] This suggests the hypothesis that: 'the primary social relation of production in the transition from traditional peasant society to industrial capitalism was established not in manufactures, but in the characteristic nexus of small and sub-peasant family economy and merchant capital.'[36] The basis of primitive accumulation can thus be seen to lie less in the expropriation of the small owner-occupier than in the channelling of merchant capital into a resilient and fairly stable peasant family economy. This approaches closely to Dobb's understanding of the problem, and to his suggestion that some small producers were able to retain a part of the surplus product for themselves, which laid the basis for 'some accumulation of capital within the petty mode of production itself, and hence for the start of a process of class differentiation within that economy of small producers'.[37]

If Marx overestimated the extent of peasant dispossession during the sixteenth century, it is important to realise that his formulation of the principle of primitive accumulation owed less to English historical examples than it did to his own observation of more recent and near-contemporary developments in Britain's periphery – to agrarian changes in post-famine Ireland and to the Scottish experience of enclosure, eviction and 'improvement' observed and elaborated by the eighteenth-century Scottish reformers and political economists. As far as Ireland was concerned, Marx believed that eviction and emigration after the famine would lead to increased proletarianisation, although recent historical work shows that eviction ceased to play a dominant role after the early 1850s, and that smallholders were able to withstand complete proletarianisation by supplementing their subsistence holdings with seasonal wage labour.[38] It was the eighteenth-century Scottish experience however, which was much more influential in shaping Marx's understanding of primitive accumulation since it was this which found a substantial place in the literature of political economy. Hobsbawm has recently suggested that Smith, Sinclair, Hume, Anderson and others may be regarded as 'the first, and one of the few examples of a bourgeoisie able to envisage its object and historic function' of replacing feudalism by capitalism or 'commercial society', and expressing its purpose in precisely these terms.[39] These men, Hobsbawm points out, were not only theorists but were also practical farmers and landowners, determined to introduce a capitalistic agriculture to the lowlands on the English pattern, and to tackle the 'highland problem', within a couple of generations. The literature which they produced was well known to Marx yet, curiously, Hobsbawm does not mention one of the most significant contributions to this debate which contains the earliest and the most complete statement of the principle of primitive accumulation, that which occurs in Sir James Steuart's *Principles of Political Oeconomy* of 1767.[40]

Steuart was a pioneer theoretician and the *Principles* may be regarded as the first comprehensive treatise on economics to use a rigorous scientific methodology, deductive as well as inductive, nine years before the *Wealth of Nations* appeared.[41] It held the stage throughout the 1770s when the debate on the future of the Highlands began. This improving landlord, however, was the advocate of a planned economy and so passionate was Smith's concern to refute his central argument that he sought to inflict 'such total defeat upon [Steuart's] system that it would vanish into oblivion.'[42] It nearly did, but Marx recognised Steuart's unique contribution to the history and theory of capital in *Theories of Surplus Value*. Although Marx hardly states this explicitly, that contribution was to delineate the basis of primitive accumulation:[43]

> His service to the theory of capital is that he shows how the process of separation takes place between the conditions of production, as the property of definite classes, and labour-power. He gives a great deal of attention to this process of the birth of capital – without as yet having the direct concept of it as capital, although he sees it as a condition for large-scale industry. He examines the process principally in agriculture; and he correctly presents the rise of manufacturing industry proper as dependent on this prior process of separation in agriculture. In Adam Smith's works this process of separation is assumed as already completed.

It is in Book I of the *Principles*, 'of Population and Agriculture', that Steuart discusses 'the Consequences which result from the Separation of the two principal Classes of a People, the Farmers and the Free Hands, with regard to their Dwelling' (chapter ten), which also contains his reflections on the backwardness of Scottish agriculture compared to England and France (chapter sixteen).[44] It was in the separation of town and countryside and in the growth of commercial agriculture with a capacity to generate food surpluses for the cities that Steuart locates economic development, 'separation . . . between the parent earth and her laborious children, which naturally takes place everywhere in proportion to the progress of industry, luxury, and the swift circulation of money.'[45] The increase of cities was regarded as a progressive development rather than a morbid outgrowth, leading to the employment of surplus labour, increase of taxable capacity, improvement of land values, and likelihood of road improvement; and the development of cottage industry was seen as regulating the level of employment in rural areas. Steuart emphasised the backwardness of Scottish farming in order to highlight the desirability of developing a capitalist agriculture or 'exchange economy', comparing the Highlands with the most poverty-stricken provinces in Europe: [46]

> Pipers, blue bonnets, and oatmeal, are known in Swabia, Auvergne, Limousin and Catalonia, as well as in Lochaber; numbers of idle, poor, useless hands, multitudes of children, whom I have found to be fed, nobody knows how, doing almost nothing at the age of fourteen, keeping of cattle and going to school, the only occupations, supposed possible for them. If you ask why they are not employed, their parents will tell you because commerce is not in the country; they talk of commerce as if it was a man, who comes to reside in some countries in order to feed the inhabitants. The truth is, it is not the fault of these poor people, but of those whose business it is to find out employment for them.

Steuart's notion of primitive accumulation was one in which commercial relations and exchange played a necessary role, proportionate to the extent of 'separation': as labourers left the land for cities, consumption in rural areas was lessened and the resulting farm surpluses were converted into money through trade. [47]

The writings of the Scottish reformers and political economists do indeed provide clear insights into the origins of primitive accumulation and the growth of capitalist agriculture, and arose directly from their own historical context, unlike Marx's account of sixteenth-century agrarian expropriation. The work of Medick and others, it may be suggested, has thrown fresh light on the relationship between merchant capital and the commercialisation of agriculture, but the fact remains that the structure of a specifically agrarian form of capitalism has rarely, if ever, been elaborated, at least with reference to England. Of course Kautsky and Lenin showed how peasant proprietorship could provide a possible alternative route to capitalism, one of slow transition; and Kautsky suggested that capitalism 'does not develop in agriculture in the simple way we thought, . . . its development is probably more complicated in this sector of the economy than in industry.' [48] This is echoed in Hobsbawm's remark that 'nobody really quite knows what we mean by capitalism in agriculture as distinct from non-

11

capitalism in agriculture . . . [since] even the most capitalist agriculture is not, as it were, a rural opposite number of the factory'.[49] Now this is precisely the point. Capitalist industry, as distinct from proto-industrialisation, has characteristically been associated with methods of production quite different from those associated with non-capitalist industry, that is, handicrafts; and these are generally capital-intensive, mechanised methods of production involving division of labour. Capitalist agriculture, on the other hand, is not easily defined in these kinds of productionist terms – if it was, it might well be indistinguishable from feudal agriculture. This is so for at least two reasons: first, productivity-raising methods in agriculture are historically much more difficult to achieve than in industry, and when they do occur are often not capital-intensive; second, food production is much more resistant than industrial production to transformation into a system of commodity production, as the history of rural unrest and food riots shows. Bearing this in mind, and recognising that the extraction of surplus value through the use of wage labour must be its essential characteristic, is it possible to suggest what constitutes the real distinctiveness of capitalist agriculture? Two additional defining characteristics seem to be important to indicate the historical moment at which a system of capitalist agriculture comes into being: first, when food production has properly become a form of commodity production, that is, has fully entered a system of commodity exchange; and second, when food supplies are appropriated and distributed without reference to customary and social controls. Both of these changes or transformations depend less upon specific methods of production and innovation than they do upon systems of exchange, marketing arrangements, and 'commercialisation'. In the nature of things, such changes are likely to be much more protracted than changes in production methods applied to industrial activities.

It can be plausibly argued that these processes in the formation of agrarian capitalism developed from the convergence between those co-existent tendencies in the late sixteenth and early seventeenth-century economy which Tawney described, and which Dobb's work supports, both analytically and chronologically: the growth of merchant capitalism and a commercialised agriculture. In the absence of accessible information however, both writers paid little attention to the historical phenomenon underlying this convergence which has dominated more recent historiography, and which Brenner, with his legitimate concern to undermine a prevalent demographic determinism, underestimates: the effects of population pressure and urbanisation, especially the growth of London.[50] Broadly speaking, the problem of a growing urban demand for foodstuffs could be met in one of two ways in sixteenth-century Europe, when the possibility of raising farming productivity was limited. Either it could be met largely by imports from abroad – as, for example, in Holland where corn was imported from the Baltic and where, consequently, merchant capitalism continued to predominate;[51] or it could be met by taking extra land into cultivation and working it with wage labour, as happened in Tudor England with the enclosure and amalgamation movement.[52] In England, it seems, the food requirements of an urban proletariat led to an intensification of rural class relations so that the commercialisation of agriculture gave way to a specifically agrarian form of capitalism, transforming the relations of production.

The most decisive changes occurred during the quarter century from 1650 to 1675. It is during this period that a specifically agrarian form of capitalism emerges, differentiated from the transitional forms that preceded it, and from the industrial capitalism which followed.[53] The abolition of feudal tenures, the abandonment of anti-enclosure legislation, the large-scale revision of rentals following Royalist land sales and repossession, the concentration of landownership into fewer hands, and a series of developments in the law which strengthened the social basis of landed property: these were the vehicles on which the new rural economy was carried. At the more fundamental level of class relations, the hardening of the so-called 'tripartite system' of landowner, tenant farmer, and wage labourer is evident following the more gradual commercialisation of agriculture which Tawney associated with the sixteenth and early seventeenth centuries. The most critical period in the history of the peasantry, it is generally agreed, occurred during the years between 1660 and 1740 which saw a substantial decline in the numbers of small owner-occupiers under the pressure of low prices and high taxation, especially burdensome during the war years from 1689 to 1713.[54]

But perhaps the most significant aspect of this series of changes, and that which has been least remarked upon, was that by which food itself became a form of property. Just as, in the sixteenth century, labour itself had become a commodity with the growth of an agrarian and industrial proletariat, so in the later seventeenth century, food production became a form of commodity production. Of course, food had been bought and sold for centuries, but these earlier transactions were regulated and hedged about by a large and surprisingly successful body of legislation attempting to control food prices, regularity of supplies, and the activities of middlemen, with the aim of securing a steady food supply. The most recent and careful investigations of government intervention in grain markets, those of R. B. Outhwaite, suggest that although 'the system was shot through with anomalies, there does exist abundant evidence of the dearth orders being operated in particular localities: of JPs forbidding the movement of corn other than to local markets; of customers and others seizing unauthorized shipments; of the local suppression of malting and brewing; of overseas imports being encouraged.[55] In the sixteenth century, government policy and popular opinion converged in expressing the Biblical view that 'He that withholdeth corn, the people shall curse him; but blessing shall be upon the head of him that selleth it.'[56] But from the 1670s, this 'policy of provision' in the interests of the poor was replaced by a policy of protection for landlords and farmers which aimed to limit supplies and raise prices through subsidised grain export during a period of depression and slow population growth.[57] By diverting grain supplies overseas, the new Corn Laws of 1672 and 1688 represented a reversal of government policy and the most vital component of a thoroughgoing form of agrarian capitalism which provoked sporadic popular protest and, from the 1750s, extensive public criticism.[58] Tawney recognised that the bounty on corn exports was quite exceptional in that it was never prefigured in any of the demands for changes in agrarian policy pressed in Parliament before the Civil War, and commented:[59]

14

The seamy side of the new order was of course the cessation of the attempt to protect the poorer classes against exploitation. The social policy of the Tudors and early Stuarts had been fitful and intermittent; but they had, at least, recognised the need for a policy, and had done more to provide one than is usually recognised. With the rapid advance after 1660 of capitalism in agriculture and industry, the need for a counterforce to the downward pressure on the weak was steadily increasing; but the old protective measures cease to be enforced, and no new measures take their place.

Again, Outhwaite's investigations provide suggestive illustration of this decisive change, in his comparison of governmental response to the harvest failures and severe shortages of the 1590s with those of the 1690s. In contrast to the situation a century earlier, the bad harvests of 1692 and 1693 passed almost without notice in the State Papers and with little sign of government action; the bad harvests of the years 1695 to 1698 likewise attracted little comment, and that mostly came from Scotland.[60] Outhwaite dates this departure in government policy from active intervention in the area of food provision from 1646 to 1650; the 1630s saw the last application of a 'dearth policy' and when the occasion arose again during the late 1640s, a parliament of landowners seemed reluctant to curb high grain prices.[61] Yet high food prices could still be accompanied, even in the late seventeenth century, by rising mortality, a phenomenon under-estimated by Appleby in his comparison of subsistence crises in England and France.[62]

The years separating the 1630s from the 1670s saw not only the State's abandonment of its role as provider of foodstuffs in times of shortage, responsible for upholding a moral economy of fair prices, but also of underlying economic realities. Slow growth or stagnation of population and food prices provided the background for a reversal of government policy, for the assumption of a passive role in relation to consumers and the poor coupled with a new responsibility for the interest of producers, that is, landowners and farmers. In the early 1670s, farmers were already complaining that grain prices were too low, and that they were unable to maintain their rent payments. The 1680s saw a run of good harvests with wheat at 34s to 35s per quarter, precisely the level at which it had stood a century earlier in spite of the intervening decades of inflation.[63] It was in these conditions of depressed prices that the first Corn Bounty Act of 1672 was passed, a policy which, according to one contemporary writer, represented 'a convention between the government and the landed interest, to which the commercial body, though materially affected by it, were not parties.'[64] The 1672 Act protected the home market by excluding imported grain and encouraged exports, in order to raise prices, by paying bounties or subsidies on all grain exported overseas. After an experimental period, the bounty was suspended, only to be re-enacted in 1688 on a permanent basis.[65] The bounty system resulted in an enormous export of grain overseas during the eighteenth century: from 1697 to 1766, over 33 million quarters of grain were exported. While the primary purpose of subsidised export was to exert an upward pressure on prices and thus maintain rent payments, its secondary purpose was to help landowners shoulder the burden of the new Land Tax, as the preamble to the 1672 Act explained: 'to the end that all owners of land whereupon this tax principally lieth may be better enabled to pay the same by rendering the labours of the husbandman in raising corn and grain more valuable by exportation of the same into foreign parts which now is already at a very low rate'.[66] The aim of the system was therefore not to maintain fair prices, but to achieve the highest market price. Basic foodstuffs were thus withdrawn from the sphere of the moral economy, and placed firmly within a system of commodity production and exchange.[67]

It is not suggested here that this policy of subsidised grain export was the only distinguishing characteristic of the new agrarian capitalism, but it was undoubtedly the most fundamental. The eighteenth-century grain export trade which it produced was neither a marginal and fluctuating surplus, nor a mere episode in English commercial history, as has sometimes been suggested, but represented a determined political intervention by the landowning class, and one in which the interests of landowners and merchants ran parallel. Hindess and Hirst observe that if a landowning class is to persist throughout the period of transition from feudalism to capitalism, the political, legal and economic conditions of their landownership must be transformed. The primary determination of their revenues will not lie only in their ability to withhold land from production, but 'in the partial determination of the level of the market price for agricultural products by the political intervention of the State.'[68]

The extent to which the bounty system actually succeeded in its primary aim of raising the level of grain prices is a difficult question which will be examined below, and one which is complicated by the apologetics of contemporary landowners who argued influentially, that the long-term effect of the bounty was, on the contrary, to reduce grain prices by increasing (or at least maintaining) the area of arable cultivation.[69] Since the trend of grain prices was undoubtedly downward during the first half of the eighteenth century, their argument sometimes appeared plausible. But, as one late eighteenth-century writer suggested, 'It would be a little surprising that any one should conceive our fathers should be such idiots as to invent a scheme to sink the value of their own estates; and more especially so at a time when they had passed an act loading themselves with a tax on those very estates of 20 p.ct.'[70] The legislation clearly *did* tend to raise prices, and was reinforced in 1737 by the passage of a statute laying down heavy penalties including hard labour, public whipping and transportation against those attempting to impede the internal movement or export of grain, and restore the moral economy of informal provision.[71]

Lord Ernle commented that men are apt to pass a hasty judgement on the Corn Laws in accordance with their political prejudices, yet in the space of a few paragraphs concluded 'it is impossible to pass any summary sentence of condemnation on the corn laws as a system selfishly designed to enrich, at the expense of consumers, a ruling class of landowning aristocrats. On the contrary . . . up to 1815, the interests alike of consumers, producers and the nation were collectively and continuously considered'.[72] T. S. Ashton on the other hand, hardly a radical historian, described the Corn Laws as a complicated body of legislation, 'the result of self-interest and prejudice'; and, 'like rulers in all ages', he wrote, 'the landlords who sat at Westminster, tended to identify the interest of the nation with that of the class to which they belonged.'[73] A balanced assessment of the effects of the Corn Laws and their place in the structure of the new agrarian capitalism is complicated by two problems. First, historians have tended towards an uncritical use of the arguments and the literature of apology constructed by contemporary landowners themselves, such as Sir Charles Smith, Arthur Young, and a series of lesser-known contributors to the *Gentleman's Magazine* and the *Farmer's Magazine*, who suggested that the effect of the Corn Laws was to increase the area of arable cultivation and to encourage agrarian improvement.[74] This line of reasoning has led modern historians towards an over-optimistic view of early eighteenth-century agriculture, which fails to explain how and why resources were forced out of a depressed and unprofitable agricultural sector, particularly arable farming, in the direction of commerce and industry, as the terms of trade between agriculture and industry shifted in favour of the latter. Even Brenner follows the optimistic path in his assessment of the early eighteenth-century agrarian economy which he suggests was marked by a 'nearly unique symbiotic relationship between agriculture and industry' involving continuing improvements in agricultural productivity combined with a dependent expansion in the home market for industrial products.[75] As J. P. Cooper commented, Prof. Brenner 'sounds like a Tory defender of the Corn Laws in his account of the fruitfulness of the partnership between capitalist farmers and beneficently far-sighted landlords.'[76] A high rate of agrarian improvement coupled with a buoyant home market forms the basis of this optimistic view of the early eighteenth-century economy, developed especially in the writings of Professor A. H. John. It is a view which minimises the extent of commercial dislocation and economic depression during these years, particularly in the second quarter of the century.[77] Since the stimulating effects of the Corn Laws are held to underpin these developments, a series of multiple advantages are credited to the grain trade, including a sizeable contribution to the balance of payments and the shipping industry, together with the undermining of the Dutch-controlled Baltic grain trade, so that 'Holland's loss was England's gain.'[78]

In the second place, the effects of the bounty legislation have been commonly estimated either by examining the evidence of prices alone, or by glancing at the aggregated export statistics relating to the grain trade, rather than by anatomising that trade, its composition, direction, organisation, and its place in European commercial relations alongside the Dutch-Baltic grain trade. It is the purpose of this study to extend the discussion in these directions and to suggest that subsidised grain export was a substantial and necessary component of agrarian capitalism in the depressed conditions of the late seventeenth and early eighteenth-century economy; and to emphasise, as Hindess and Hirst have done, that the Corn Laws should be seen not merely as an economic mechanism or regulator, but as a considered intervention at the political level. Dr Black has investigated the political consequences of the grain trade during the 1730s, and has shown a clear relationship between British neutrality in the War of the Polish Succession and the need to protect the grain trade, as well as the Government's sensitivity to the degree of support needed from the grain-producing areas during the elections of 1734, bearing in mind the agricultural interests of the Walpoles in Norfolk, the Duke of Grafton in Suffolk, and the Duke of Newcastle in Sussex.[79] Indeed, the history of the grain trade shows an uneasy accommodation of interest between landlords and merchants which represented an increasingly close defensive alliance, in both political and economic terms, between farming and commerce. In the United Provinces on the other hand, the grain trade remained under the control of narrowly mercantile interests which were complementary to those of industry, mainly the 'verkeersindustrien' or processing industries. In Britain, a strong antagonism prevailed between industrial interests and the agrarian-mercantile interest in the grain trade, especially from brewers, distillers and maltsters, forcibly expressed from the 1750s onwards, long before the celebrated struggle over the early nineteenth-century Corn Laws began. Yet within this landowning/grain-growing/mercantile nexus, there could be no clearer illustration of the notion of an agrarian class, both of rentiers and entrepreneurs, as an authentic bourgeoisie – a notion which some Marxist writers have found difficult to accept.[80]

Sir James Steuart, whose early formulation of the origins of primitive accumulation has already been noticed, attached great importance to what he termed 'the industry of man' in establishing agriculture. Nature, he believed, provided man with 'a small sum [which] sets him a-going, but it is his industry [in establishing agriculture] which makes the fortune';[81] and in a passage which anticipates Malthus, he suggests that the plenty or scarcity of food determines the size of the population.[82] Steuart was unambiguous in arguing for a flourishing commercial agriculture, and devoted one complete and well-informed chapter and several passages in the *Principles* to discussion of the grain export trade.[83] But he was singular in his clear opposition to a policy of forced grain export, favouring instead one of cheap food and stable grain prices regulated through a system of public granaries for domestic supply only. The 'keeping food cheap, and still more the preserving it at all times at an equal standard', he observed, 'is the fountain of the wealth of Holland; and . . . any hurtful competition in this article must beget a disorder which will affect the whole of the manufacturers of a state.'[84] In a more explicit statement, Steuart explodes the contemporary myth that the existence of an export trade in grain proved that the entire population was well fed, and that grain export did not, therefore, restrain the growth of population:

> I answer, that [the growth of population] is still stopt for want of food, for the exportation marks only that the home demand is satisfied; but this does not prove that the inhabitants are full fed, although they can buy no more at the exportation price. Those who cannot buy, are exactly those who I say die for want of subsistence; could they buy, they would live and multiply, and no grain perhaps would be exported. This is a plain consequence of my reasoning; and my principal point in view, throughout this whole book, is to find out a method for enabling the indigent to buy up this very quantity which is at present exported.'[85]

Steuart understood better than most of his contemporaries the historical circumstances which had produced a developing capitalist agriculture in Britain, in which the old policy of provision was being replaced by one of protection and foodstuffs drawn into the sphere of commodity exchange. In advocating a degree of central planning to restore the level of fair and stable prices, he was either behind the times or substantially ahead of them, and was in any case writing when the grain export trade was coming to an end so that his strictures soon seemed anachronistic. But he realised that the Corn Laws expressed little of that paternalistic concern for the consumer with which their apologists often credited them. Edward Thompson is right to suggest that 'the abrogation of the old moral economy of "provision" was not the work of an industrial bourgeoisie but of capitalist farmers, improving landlords, and great millers and corn-merchants',[86] but it needs to be emphasised that this work began with the experimental Corn Law of 1672 as a system of price supports for producers, not with the publication of the *Wealth of Nations* almost a century later.

II The Grain Trade anatomised, 1700–1760

Writing in the *Farmer's Magazine* for 1802, Dr George Skene Keith, author of one of the Board of Agriculture's county reports, surveyed the rise, progress and decline of the English grain trade during the previous century.[1] The course of that trade, he considered, fell naturally into three equal and distinct periods, as the statistics of the Inspector General of Imports and Exports showed:

Table 1: Grain Trade of England and Wales, 1697–1801 (million quarters)

		Exports	Imports	Excess Exports (+)/ Imports (−)
1697–1731	Wheat	3.59	0.13	+3.46
	Malt & Barley	7.47	0.04	+7.43
	Oats & Rye	1.32	0.61	+0.71
1732–1766	Wheat	11.54	0.29	+11.25
	Malt & Barley	10.26	0.05	+10.21
	Oats & Rye	1.80	1.07	+0.73
1767–1801	Wheat	3.06	10.54	−7.48
	Malt & Barley	2.61	1.96	+0.65
	Oats & Rye	0.90	16.04	−15.14

Source: PRO: Customs 3

As far as the first period of moderate exports was concerned, Skene Keith thought it was necessary to point out that this was a 'period of national economy; that our agriculture had a much inferior population to support; and that the bounty which had recently been given by Parliament no doubt stimulated our exportation, which had formerly been loaded with a duty.' During the second period, from 1732 to 1766, the trade grew to substantial proportions and these years, according to Skene Keith, were 'distinguished by national industry, and also by economy rather than luxury. The population was not much increased; only a small quantity of oats was consumed on horses; and not a great demand for barley, either by the distiller or the common brewer . . . the seasons in general had been more favourable, and crops more abundant.' During the 1760s, grain exports were overtaken by imports and the last three decades of the century formed a period of substantial net imports. This third period, Keith emphasised, 'was distinguished by a great increase of population, a very improved mode of agriculture, and a high degree of national exertion stimulated by a national spirit of enterprise, a great accumulation of capital, and also by our national luxury and profusion. Notwithstanding which, we have imported an immense quantity of corn (nearly one year's supply), in the course of the last 35 years.'[2]

This near-contemporary account of the grain trade is interesting in that it places most emphasis on the effects of the bounty and the absence of population growth in encouraging exports, together with the added stimulus of good seasons during the years of most substantial export. Significantly, agricultural improvement does not play an important part in this brief analysis, being associated with the later years of the century in the shape of 'a very improved mode of agriculture.' The relative importance of these varied influences will be examined below, but it is first necessary to disaggregate the trade into its component parts, recognising that different grains were affected by different sources of demand, and bearing in mind Skene Keith's chronology.

At the outset, it must be emphasised that the bread grains – wheat, rye and oatmeal – were exported as foodstuffs either to the granaries of Holland for both domestic consumption and international redistribution, or directly to European markets, particularly those of the south, during periods of scarcity; while malt and barley were exported as industrial raw materials for the supply of brewers and distillers, especially those of Holland. This important distinction, which is also reflected in the organisation of the grain trade, emerges strikingly from the Inspector General's trade statistics, from which the trends shown in figures 1–3 have been derived.[3] The official trade statistics provide a reasonable indication of the real volume of grain shipments, and any errors that may exist are largely attributable to merchants' over-entries made in order to claim excess subsidies. Examination of the Customs Letter Books shows that such practices were limited in scope until the 1740s and early 1750s when supervision at the waterside became more lax as a result of the substantially increased volume of shipments.[4] Figures for these years may therefore be somewhat exaggerated, though this is unlikely to affect the relative proportions of the different grains exported.[5]

The first two phases identified by Skene Keith in the history of the eighteenth-century grain trade are clearly reflected in the trends shown in figure 1. At the same time, there is the suggestion of a significant qualitative difference between these two periods which was not remarked upon by that writer.[6] The first thirty years of the century were characterised by a low and stable level of exports of bread grains – wheat, rye, and oatmeal – and the overall trend of grain exports was determined by the considerably greater volume of malt and barley exports. During the second period of more substantial export, this position was reversed, with the overall trend determined by the greater volume of wheat, rye, and oatmeal shipments. It will be shown that adjustments to the export subsidies played a major part in shaping changes in the composition of the trade between the two periods.

Figures 2 and 3 indicate another salient characteristic of the trade: the importance of Holland as the largest single market for English grain. This had been noted by Davenant in 1711, who complained that the Dutch had 'too great a share in a plentiful year of corn here'.[7] If it seemed that England was displacing the Baltic countries as the cornfield of Europe, it was nevertheless apparent that Holland still remained its granary. 'It is true,' wrote Defoe in 1728, 'that dear or cheap, corn always finds a market in Holland; but 'tis as true, that if the Dutch find a forced exportation, they, like all expert merchants, will buy cheap and perhaps to loss . . . in short it is no market at all.'[8] In fact, the official trade statistics (figures 2

24

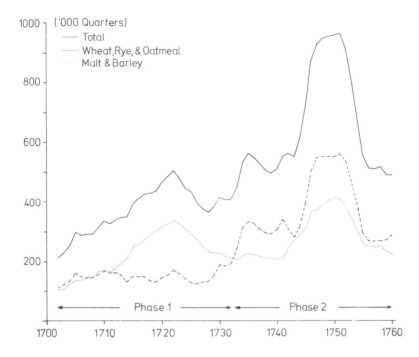

Figure 1: English Grain Exports, 1700–60 (nine year moving averages)
Sources: PRO: Customs 3
Customs House, London: Customs Ledgers

and 3) show that Holland's apparent predominance as a market for English grain was largely confined to the first phase of export (1697–1731) during which malt and barley dominated the trade, since the Dutch market always absorbed a far higher proportion of English malt and barley than of the bread grains. More precisely, between 10 and 45 per cent of England's surplus wheat, rye and oatmeal was sent to Holland annually, while over 75 per cent of malt and barley exports were annually disposed of in this way until the proportion fell in the late 1740s and early 1750s. In 1751, this represented one-third of Holland's total wheat and rye imports, one-

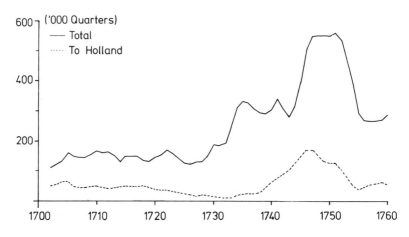

Figure 2: English Exports of Wheat, Rye, and Oatmeal, 1700–60 (nine year moving averages)

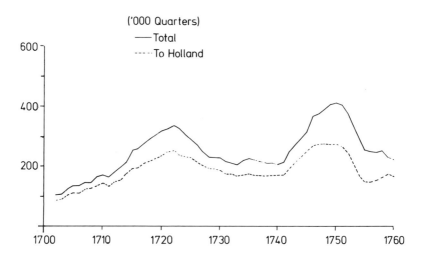

Figure 3: English Exports of Malt and Barley, 1700–60 (nine year moving averages)

Sources: PRO: Customs 3
      Customs House, London: Customs Ledgers

half of its total barley imports, and almost all its total malt imports.[9]

As one might expect, the trade in bread grains to Holland was more sensitive to wartime conditions than was the case with the malt and barley trade, and during periods of peace, the former was only of marginal significance. During the first twenty years of the eighteenth century, exports of bread grains to Holland fluctuated around 50,000 quarters annually, only to decline steadily throughout the 1720s to the low levels of the 1730s. During the War of the Austrian Succession however, the Dutch market revived considerably when exports of bread grains reached levels of over 150,000 quarters. At this time, the British Army was supplied from Holland and this situation, together with trading difficulties brought about by war, goes some way towards explaining why the proportion of bread grains exported to Holland rose substantially.[10] Various circumstances unconnected with wartime conditions also had a bearing on the situation, such as the short-term difficulties facing Dutch farmers and the availability and prices of alternative supplies, especially from the Baltic, and these kinds of considerations will be discussed in due course. None the less it remains true that in the grain trade, as in a number of other branches of Anglo-Dutch trade, the redistributive functions of the Dutch market revived during wartime as direct trade between England and southern Europe became difficult. In 1739 for example, a Newcastle merchant wrote to his Rotterdam correspondent: 'We would have a very brisk corn export for the Portugal and Spanish markets, but since our masters have got a notion of Spanish privateers being out they won't go any way to the southward.'[11] When peace returned, the markets of Southern Europe, principally Spain, Portugal, and the Straits of Gibraltar, regained their previously predominant position in this branch of the trade.[12]

The export of malt and barley to Holland, being less subject to the artificial stimulus of war, followed a more stable course than exports of bread grains. While malt and barley exports to Europe as a whole indeed rose significantly during the War of the Austrian Succession, the proportion sent to Holland actually declined, and this serves to emphasise the fact that these grains were sent to

27

Holland for industrial use rather than for storage and redistribution to other European countries as was the case with bread grains. Two constant features of this branch of trade should be emphasised at the outset. In the first place, malt was always exported in greater quantities than barley for fiscal reasons, usually in proportions greater than 4:1. In the second place, Norfolk and the ports of Yarmouth, and to a lesser extent Wells and Lynn, were of overwhelming national predominance in the trade because of the extent of the grain-producing hinterland and the accessibility of the Dutch market.[13] As some of the opponents of the bounty system were later to argue, the temptation to ship grain to Holland in preference to the home market was strong in view of the short sea voyage and the low cost of water transport for a bulky commodity sensitive to handling charges.[14] Carriage by sea, it was estimated in the late seventeenth century, was generally twenty times cheaper than carriage by land: a calculation which Professor Willan feels is 'little exaggerated'.[15] Of the two groups of Dutch 'consumers' of English malt and barley, the brewers and the distillers, the latter took by far the larger share since most brewers already operated their own malt-houses; and the Dutch distilleries were indeed highly accessible to the East Anglian ports. By 1771, when the location of the mature distilling industry had been fully worked out, it was apparent that of the 200 distilleries in Holland, 122 were located at Schiedam, 22 at Rotterdam, and 22 at Delftshaven.[16] In other words 83 per cent of all distilleries in Holland were to be found in the Maas region where the bulk of English trade was already concentrated. The malt and barley trade therefore possessed a notably regional character, connecting two well defined areas on either side of the North Sea. During the second and third decades of the century when the business of malting and malt export was subject to much discussion, the arguments of maltsters and merchants emerged as a distinctly regional issue.

If English merchants and maltsters were encouraged, under the stimulus of bounties and other inducements, to export to the nearby market of Holland, Dutch distillers were equally keen to take what was in effect a subsidised product. It is worthwhile, therefore, to examine the nature of the subsidies themselves. The provisions of the 1688 bounty legislation are well known: bounties were granted of 5*s* per quarter of wheat exported overseas when the home price did not exceed 48*s*; 3*s* 6*d* for rye when the price did not exceed 32*s*; and 2*s* 6*d* for malt and barley when the price did not exceed 24*s*.[17] Apart from temporary suspensions, these levels remained in force until the adjustments of 1772/3.[18] In addition to the bounty, the export of malt was further encouraged by a drawback of the malt duty during the first quarter of the eighteenth century,[19] and by exemption from duty after 1726.[20] Modern writers on the grain trade have consistently emphasised the stimulating effects of the bounty system on exports, particularly wheat, but have failed to recognise the twofold stimulus which lay behind the growing volume of malt exports from the early years of the century. This is all the more surprising since the bounty represented a less substantial fiscal incentive than the drawback, which cancelled out a heavy duty. From 1697 to 1760, a duty of 6*d* was to be paid by the maltster for every bushel of malt paid (i.e. 4*s* per quarter); but the whole of this sum could be 'drawn back' or reclaimed if the malt was exported overseas. The purpose of the drawback, as one reliable commercial writer suggested, was to 'enable the English merchant to furnish the Southern parts of the Province of Holland, and other countries as cheap, or cheaper, than those of Amsterdam could do with the malt they make of the barley imported from the Baltic.[21] To the extent that the provisions of the act achieved this result, this was as much due to evasion and manipulation of the excise regulations by exporting maltsters, as to anything which Parliament had been able to devise.

Because bounties and drawbacks were paid on the basis of bulk rather than weight, exporting maltsters contrived to produce a bulkier product than they otherwise might have done, by manipulating the excise regulations which attempted to control the extent to which barley was allowed to swell and germinate during the malting process.[22] The Excise Office claimed in 1717 that it had become a common practice for exporting maltsters to allow their barley to sprout and grow 'excessively' as it lay on the malthouse floor, following the steeping and germination stages. In this way, it was alleged, maltsters were able to convert twenty bushels of barley into thirty bushels of malt and obtain a 'bonus' drawback on the excess ten bushels. The excise officers were obliged to grant an allowance of ten bushels in every twenty to account for shrinkage,[23] but maltsters were able to 'almost entirely prevent' shrinkage taking place. Furthermore, bounties were claimed, and paid, in proportion to the amount of drawback. This practice, it was said in 1717, was chiefly carried on in Norfolk where it was 'much increased of late years', but was beginning to spread to other counties.[24] The predominance of Norfolk was reflected in the drawback figures quoted by the Excise Office two years later: around 90 per cent of all drawbacks paid on malt exports were claimed by Norfolk exporters during the years 1716 to 1719.[25] Similar accusations were made of a more exaggerated kind by the brewers who were to a limited extent competing for the same raw materials as maltsters.[26] 'Barley was steeped so as to increase eight or ten times in measure', it was alleged, 'and being exported under the name of malt, received bounty on that quantity.'[27] This was the 'bogus-malt' which probably figured more prominently in the polemical literature surrounding the conflict between the revenue authorities and the maltsters than it did in reality.

In their anxiety to protect the revenue, the customs and excise authorities tended to ignore the technical requirements of the Dutch distillers for whom the bulk of Norfolk malt exports were destined. Indeed, the Excise Office described the latter as a 'commodity of little or no value, which can make little or no returns from foreign parts.'[28] But in fact the 'blowing-up' of barley by East Anglian maltsters produced the 'long-malt' with a high enzyme content which was necessary for the distilling of Dutch *genever*.[29] The composition of long malt was such that it broke down the large quantities of unmalted grain with which it was mixed in the initial stages of production. Some Yarmouth exporters, it seems, were in effect undertaking this preliminary stage of production by exporting a mixture of long malt and unmalted grain which, because of the extra bulk created, could be a highly profitable operation through the additional bounties claimed.[30] In 1714, for example, the Collector of Customs at Yarmouth sent a sample of Norfolk malt to the Commissioners of Trade in London, asking them to note the 'foulness and dross therein, whereof there is great quantities shipd from hence, tho' some shipd off is of a better sort.'[31] From a mixture of malted and unmalted grain, crude malt spirits (*moutwijn*) were produced which were redistilled (or 'rectified') with the flavour of juniper berries. These two basic processes were in fact separately organised: malt was purchased by the distillers of Schiedam to be converted into crude spirits, which was then sold on the *Moutwijnbeurs* at Schiedam (established in 1718) to the wine merchants of Rotterdam who undertook redistillation and organised export to France, England and Spain.[32] As Combrune explained, the Dutch were able to make good the defects of cheap English malt and 'ever attentive to their interests, soon found on what easy conditions their distilleries might be maintained.'[33] Here, it seemed, was the mercantilist's case of a damaging trade – one which resulted in the loss of potentially useful raw materials to the advantage of a competitor's manufacturing industry. Certainly, the cheapness of subsidised English malt and barley was its prime attraction, and one of the Government's diplomatic agents had seen these grains sold in Rotterdam 'for little more than an honest maltster in England could prepare it, or the farmer get it into his barn', and ascribed this to the unintended effects of the drawback.[34] No doubt the exporting maltster obtained his profit chiefly at the expense of the public revenue, but the point could be made that the trade opened up a market for inferior barleys which were most suitable for 'blowing-up' and in the words of the maltster were 'fittest for a foreign market'.[35]

As far as the revenue authorities were concerned however, a situation had arisen in which maltsters were obtaining higher drawback and bounty payments than the legislature had intended and, in many instances, this actually amounted to fraudulent practice.[36] An attempt was made in 1720 to remedy these abuses with the passage of an act which was possibly drafted by the Excise Office and which attempted to prohibit excessive 'acrospiring', that is, the swelling of the acrospire or shoot of the grain.[37] This was apparently difficult to define or enforce, particularly in view of the fact that long malt (malt with a long 'acrospire') was technically necessary for Dutch distillers. Six years later therefore, the drawback was totally withdrawn and all malt intended for export was in future to pay no duty in the first place.[38] In spite of the degree of forward planning on the part of maltsters and exporters which this necessitated, the 1726 act seems to have worked reasonably well. Complaints were occasionally received from the Commissioners of Customs that the quantity of malt entered on an excise certificate did not agree with the quantity entered on the debenture (relating to malt actually exported), but this could easily be explained by local conditions.[39] Each maltster might make thirty, forty or fifty steepings of malt in a season, all of which would be placed in his warehouse under a joint lock with the excise officer.[40] Although individual withdrawals from this stock might not tally with the excise certificates, the officers were satisfied provided that an overall balance was obtained at the end of the season.[41] This appears to have been well understood at Yarmouth which handled a high proportion of all malt exports. When we turn to the statistics of malt and barley exports to Holland, the obvious decline after 1726 seems to suggest that the act of that year was fairly successful in curtailing the worst excesses of exporting maltsters, and by implication it confirms some of the accusations which had been levelled against them earlier. The years 1728 and 1729 were, of course, marked by dearth and high prices so that we would in any case expect some decline in exports, but it is clear that this is already under way in 1727:

Table 2: Malt and Barley Exports to Holland, 1720–30
('000 quarters)

1720	163.6	1726	276.1
1721	265.3	1727	186.7
1722	294.2	1728	177.6
1723	236.6	1729	128.5
1724	222.5	1730	160.5
1725	258.4		

Source: PRO: Customs 3

The act of 1726, therefore, made that of 1720 (attempting to control 'acrospiring') somewhat redundant. The bounty on exported malt still continued so that some incentive remained to 'blow-up' barley, but withdrawal of the drawback had reduced this considerably. In 1730, the provisions of the 1720 act relating to 'acrospiring' were repealed, and a fixed ratio was statutorily established between the quantity of barley steeped and the output of malt produced.[42] But there is no evidence to suggest that these proportions were strictly adhered to: by 1738, it was reported that 'malt for Holland markets . . . in making is suffered to run out to a very great length on the floors', and in 1741 that 20 quarters of barley were made into 38 or 40 quarters of malt.[43] It seems, therefore, that the remarkable growth of English malt exports during the first quarter of the eighteenth century (and possibly beyond) owed little to the natural competitiveness of the malting industry, but proceeded rather from quite adventitious circumstances, namely, the manipulation of fiscal incentives which in some instances involved fraudulent practice. However the conjuncture of the English malt legislation with the technical requirements of Dutch distillers produced, on the supply side, a flow of heavily subsidised raw materials whose expansion was self-reinforcing given that the demand for Dutch spirits was highly elastic. Certainly, the English agent in Rotterdam had no doubt that Dutch distillers had a 'constant vent for as much spirits as they could make' during the first half of the eighteenth century when 'almost all the distillers and most part of the brewers used to depend upon England for malt.'[44] It is hardly surprising then, that the period which saw the most rapid growth of the Dutch distilling industry coincided with that of the English bulk export of malt and barley.

III Commercial Organisation

It has already been shown that, as industrial raw materials, malt and barley were subject to different sources of overseas demand than was the case with the bread grains. In addition, malt was affected by its own peculiar supply characteristics in the shape of processing. Not surprisingly, these distinctions between the two branches of the grain trade were reflected in its organisation.

As far as malting for the domestic market is concerned, it is fairly clear that the industry during the eighteenth century was substantially dominated by the Common Brewer – with the exception of London where the size of the market and lack of space encouraged specialisation between brewers and maltsters. Professor Mathias has shown how provincial malting and brewing remained allied under the same management and at the same site, although some independent maltsters carried on their trade by supplying a variety of customers, especially household brewers.[1] In Norfolk, malting and brewing had already become integrated by the end of the seventeenth century, as the Norwich merchant Thomas Baret explained to Sir Josiah Child: 'Malting and grazing were very Genteele imployments for Gentlemen's younger sons . . . both which ways are now quite lost as to the profit of them, viz. the brewers have joined malting to their other trade & now will buy no malt but use what (they) makes & so the maltsters for want of customers was forced to give over'. In the face of a contracting demand from local brewers therefore, it is only to be expected that Norfolk maltsters who produced for the export trade were relieved of the need to compete with the organised brewing maltsters for raw materials, since the 'long malt' required by the Dutch distillers could be made from the cheapest and inferior grades of barley. As Thomas Baret went on to explain, the brewing maltsters 'combine together & give but what price they please, & when they have a little before hand will bring corn from 10*s* to 6*s* p. coomb & under in less than two months time by pretending they want none, when if their chambers were examined, they are not half stockt for the year'.[2] The terms of trade were thus becoming increasingly disadvantageous for independent maltsters, and while market conditions did not amount to those of complete monopsony (domination of the market by a single buyer), this was at least the direction in which change was occurring.

It seems, therefore, that structural changes were taking place in the malting industry which, together with the attractions of bounties and drawbacks, must have made the export trade irresistable to independent maltsters, and some of them became heavily committed to it. In the 1730s for example, John Wright of Honingham, near Norwich, kept five malt houses employed for the export trade alone.[3] In this, and probably the majority of instances, production and export were organised separately. In 1730 the Collector of Customs at Yarmouth reported that 'a good deal of malt is sent out of the country by the country maltsters to our merchants to export for them' – merchants such as Joseph Cox who a few years later was described as agent for several maltsters, some of whom lived more than twenty miles from the port.[4] But at the same time, it seems that a certain proportion of the malt trade was handled by merchants exporting on their own accounts. Norwich merchants in the 1750s, for example, were themselves buying barley and making the arrangements for malting, in which case they remained the owners of the grain during the malting process.[5] It is not possible to be much more precise as to the relative proportions of the trade handled by merchants exporting on their own accounts and by maltsters' agents, and it seems likely that some individuals combined both activities. Nevertheless, the numbers engaged in the trade, whether as agents or exporters, were fairly small, and one or two names dominate the Yarmouth Port Books. In 1737 for example, fifteen people entered quantities of malt for export overseas but only six of these entered more than 3000 quarters, as shown in Table 3. It is likely that this handful of men were agents for country maltsters (and Cox at the head of the list appears in the Customs

Table 3: Merchants and Agents exporting Malt
from Yarmouth, 1737

	quantity exported '000 quarters	*percentage shipped to Rotterdam*	*percentage of Yarmouth's total malt exports*
J. Cox	8.14	89.4	14.1
T. Martin	7.52	84.9	13.0
R. Jarvis	7.00	68.5	12.1
R. Boyce	8.47	55.7	14.6
G. Ward	5.26	66.1	9.1
C. Benard	3.27	70.8	5.6
9 others	18.22	—	31.5

Sources: Exchequer K.R. Port Books, E. 190/551/13
Treasury Miscellanea, T. 64/277

Letter Books as such, though Jarvis was referred to in 1731 as a merchant shipping *his* malt directly from the kiln).[6] The trade of this small group of Yarmouth exporters and agents accounted for almost one-third of total English malt exports, and just over two-thirds of Yarmouth's malt trade. The destination of the bulk of these shipments was, of course, Rotterdam.

The Yarmouth Port Books indicate another salient characteristic of the grain export trade: the marked specialisation which existed between exporters of malt and bread grains. The above-named agents and merchants were concerned almost exclusively with malt. Wheat and rye were handled by a different group of exporters (or agents), chiefly Messrs White, Olier and Palgrave. The last-mentioned, for example, shipped 13,205 quarters of wheat to overseas markets in 1737 (of which 5810 quarters went to Rotterdam), while he shipped only 432 quarters of malt.[7] This further emphasises the distinction between these two groups of grains: not only were they absorbed by different markets and put to different uses, they might be handled by virtually separate groups of exporters within a single region.

The trade in bread grains was much less regionally concentrated than the malt trade, with supplies drawn from the southern and eastern counties, often by way of London, and distributed to a wider range of European markets. Some idea of the regional origins of grain exports may be gained by comparing the contributions of the outports, and this is shown in Table 4. The fact that a high proportion of bread grains passed through the wholesale markets of London means that comparisons based on the export statistics alone tend to obscure the real contributions of the grain-producing areas. Nevertheless, the increasing role of London in the handling of cereal exports between the 1730s and the succeeding two decades deserves notice, parallelled only by the increasing contribution of the East Anglian ports. Organisation of the wholesale grain markets of London was rationalised at mid-century when the corn factors abandoned their Monday, Wednesday and Saturday markets by the waterside at Bear Quay and entered the fine new Corn Factors' Exchange in nearby Mark Lane. Completed in 1751, the new Exchange was open for daily business. 'There they fingered their little palmsful of grain and bargained under less draughty circumstances in the coffee houses on the upper floor.'[8] These new arrangements – more commodious but less democratic than the old – would scarcely have been possible without a prior series of accumulated 'improvements' in internal marketing which made the metropolitan market more accessible to provincial suppliers: the growing practice of selling on the basis of samples, the regular publication of London prices in the provincial press, and intensified competition among the owners of coasting vessels, the corn hoys, which lowered freight charges.[9]

From the standpoint of commercial organisation, it must be emphasised that London merchants and factors exercised an even more dominant influence over the trade in bread grains than the data of Table 4 would indicate. While much grain was indirectly exported to Europe via the granaries of London, substantial amounts were also exported from the outports on the accounts of London merchants. In 1714/15 for example, the prominent Hull merchants Nathaniel and Henry Maister were engaged as factors to several London merchants, completing wheat cargoes of between

Table 4: English and Welsh Ports Exporting Grain, 1736–63

Percentage of grain exported from:	1736–39		1744–48		1749–53		1754–58		1759–63	
	Malt & Barley	Wheat Rye & Oatmeal	Malt & Barley	Wheat Rye & Oatmeal	Malt & Barley	Wheat Rye & Oatmeal	Malt & Barley	Wheat Rye & Oatmeal	Malt & Barley	Wheat Rye & Oatmeal
North East	3.9	17.7	2.4	14.7	2.4	15.5	0.7	5.8	3.3	12.2
East Anglia	81.9	17.1	83.6	38.4	77.6	28.4	79.3	31.2	84.9	32.4
London	3.9	17.1	0.8	23.5	3.1	30.7	0.6	27.7	1.9	32.2
South East	1.9	12.0	4.4	7.3	6.5	9.2	8.2	11.3	3.6	5.3
South	2.1	9.0	2.2	8.3	5.6	8.1	9.5	7.6	4.9	13.8
South West	5.3	7.4	4.3	5.4	3.4	5.4	1.5	14.7	0.4	3.0
Wales	0.8	0.6	1.6	1.6	1.0	1.3	0.1	0.5	0.7	0.6
North West	0.2	0.9	0.7	0.8	0.4	1.4	0.1	1.2	0.3	0.5

Sources: 1736–39, Gentleman's Magazine, XII & XIII
1744–63, BM: Add. Ms. 38387

400 and 900 quarters (each for the account of a single merchant) to be shipped from Hull and consigned to agents in Amsterdam, Lisbon and Hamburg for which the customary 2 per cent commission was charged.[10] During the 1730s while representing Hull in Parliament, Henry took advantage of his business connections in the Commons to secure large commissions from London merchants which were passed on to Nathaniel in Hull to be completed with northern grain.[11] Since it was acknowledged that 'if a man ingages [in corn] by way of commission, it will infallibly take up his whole attendance upon Bear Key', we might suppose that Henry Maister devoted more attention to the corn trade than he did to politics.[12] Early in 1738, for example, he had obtained a commission for 6500 quarters of wheat to be shipped from Hull to Cadiz on the account of John Bance, MP for Westbury in Wiltshire. At the same time, the Maister brothers were exporting grain on their own accounts chiefly to Lisbon, Cadiz and Amsterdam. Given the combined extent of their own business and their substantial commission sales, it is hardly surprising that they encountered difficulties in obtaining sufficient shipping and in assembling bulk shipments of uniform quality and price. In March 1738 for example, Nathaniel wrote from Hull, 'It comes in prodigious slowly; tho' I have given 2 or 3 of the factors permission to go along with the market price, I don't find they buy any. I have got about 70 quarters since my last advice that the whole of what we have bought is about 5,500 (quarters). If the price was one fixed, it would come in plentiful enough as there are great quantities yet in the country.'[13] During an earlier year for which information is available, 1714, it appears that the Maisters obtained their grain from at least twenty-three separate farmers and country factors.[14] Success rested among other things on purchasing at the beginning of the year before 'the buyers begin to stir', or just after harvest when farmers needed cash to purchase livestock.[15] As one merchant wrote during October, 'our fair is just now and country men must have their money to buy their cattle.'[16]

Ralph Carr of Newcastle provides another example of a provincial merchant who was 'pretty deeply engaged . . . in the corn trade for export', and who maintained close links with the London grain market chiefly, it seems, to supply its factors at times when the difference between home and overseas prices did not encourage export. To a correspondent who had recommended Messrs J. and T. Simpson of London, Carr replied, 'they shall have a large share of my business at Bear Key for tho' I am pretty closely attached to some factors there, yet I am under no considerable obligation to any of them.'[17] As well as exporting grain on his own account and supplying the London export market, Carr also undertook commissions for overseas buyers. 'We have at present a very large demand from France, Spain, Portugal and Barbary', he wrote in November 1738, and '... I have very large quantities of wheat bought up and fresh orders arriving every day'.[18] Although documentation is sparse, the indications are that the larger exporters did not adopt a uniform method of trading, but combined the functions of exporting merchant with that of corn factor as occasion demanded. Even the smaller country factors might export on their own accounts. In 1740 the customs officers noticed a quantity of wheat shipped from Sunderland to Amsterdam which was the joint property of a coal fitter and a corn factor.[19]

The scale of operations could vary enormously within the trade from the small and usually speculative shipments of general merchants to the substantial quantities of grain handled by the navy victualling contractors (assembling 4000 quarters of wheatmeal alone per month in the 1750s) or by the London factors such as Thomas Farrer, who claimed to have shipped off 40,000 quarters in one year.[20] But the 'largest and most adventurous corn dealers' in the Kingdom were said to be the Coutts brothers of London and Edinburgh who established an elaborate network of factors throughout Scotland and England to supply their extensive export trade. It is described in some detail by the firm's nineteenth-century historian:[21]

> They had a settled agent in Northumberland, residing at Fenwick, who was employed to make purchases of corn for the house, and for none else, in that country. Others at Aberdeen, at Portsoy, and at Dundee, made purchases for the house in the fertile corn countries of Perth, Forfar, Kincardine, Aberdeen, Banff, and Moray; and two others again, in Caithness and in Ross-shire, both of them gentlemen of landed

property, but also men of business, though not, strictly speaking, merchants, made purchases for the house on their joint account in those northern counties. In England the house had large quantities of corn shipped for them at Yarm and at Stockton in Yorkshire; at Lynn Regis, Fakenham, and Yarmouth all in the rich county of Norfolk; at Haverfordwest, in South Wales; and by the noted Cooper Thornhill, who at the time kept the Bell Inn at Hilton, and was one of the most considerable corn factors in England.

None of these specialist exporters was wholly committed to the grain trade however. The unpredictability of harvests and the level of prices, the possibility of overheating and damage during storage and transit, and the relatively high cost of handling and therefore of transhipment, meant that the trade was extremely risky and speculative. During periods of harvest failure, exports could be reduced to low levels or could disappear altogether following an embargo. Thus the Couttses combined their primary interest in grain with trade in lead, salt and tobacco before their banking activities grew to predominance in the later part of the century.[22] Ralph Carr exported flax, lead, litharge and coal as well as grain, and the Maisters operated a very extensive trade with Scandinavia and the Baltic.[23] But just as these large grain exporters tended to diversify their interests, so the general merchant might occasionally enter this somewhat specialised branch of trade, in which case his consignment would probably be sent to Amsterdam to be sold on commission by a Dutch House. The Amsterdam grain market with its weekly quotations of English wheat, rye, barley and malt prices published in the *Amsterdamsche Prijscouranten* was probably less unfamiliar than the fluctuating markets of southern Europe.[24] Small and irregular shipments however were unlikely to yield satisfactory returns and it seems that the greatest profits would be made by those merchants shipping grain in bulk directly to final markets. Apart from tending towards reduced unit handling charges, bulk shipment permitted the exporter to charter a vessel and thus to secure a quick despatch and retain complete discretion over the final disposal of the cargo, which would eliminate some of the risk caused by fluctuating markets. Charter-parties in the Rotterdam notarial archives relating to English grain shipments show that masters trading to Southern Europe were frequently given instructions to lie for twenty-four hours at either Lisbon or Cadiz 'to await orders whether to sail to Gibraltar, Malaga, Cartagena, Alicante, Barcelona, Cette, Marseilles, Toulon or Genoa.'[25] Specialist exporters usually received fairly precise reports of price changes and differentials in various markets. In 1740, for example, Ralph Carr was expecting to load five grain ships for Holland and 'sundry more' for southern Europe and at this time was corresponding regularly with agents in a number of grain markets: T. M. Liebenrood in Rotterdam and J. A. Crop in Amsterdam providing information on the state of Dutch Market; William Hayes in Konigsberg on Baltic supplies; William Norton in Dunkirk on western and northern French markets (Nantes, La Rochelle and Rouen) and unnamed correspondents in southern France and Lisbon.[26] The most important of these correspondents was undoubtedly Liebenrood in Rotterdam who also provided information on the extent and direction of Baltic supplies, particularly those destined for Holland. In May 1738, for example, he wrote to Liebenrood 'please inform me how the demand & prices of corn goes with you & your opinion. Barley as well as wheat is much advanced and there is like to be an export of that grane for the Spanish and Portugal marketts . . . please likewise to let me know if there is much corn either already come or exported to your parts from the Baltic.'[27] Liebenrood's reply that large quantities of Baltic grain were expected caused Carr to look towards the Spanish and Portuguese rather than the Dutch Market.[28] And in the later part of 1740 when scarcity at home had transformed the grain export trade into an import trade, Carr circumvented the Dutch granaries and despatched ships direct to Danzig; in addition, he called upon his Dutch intermediary to supply information as to grain already in transit from the East country, but explained that he was unwilling to purchase such grain after it had been landed in Holland.[29] Carr was obviously anxious to avoid excessive handling and reshipment charges which import via Holland would involve: handling charges, commission and import fees on foreign grain imported into Amsterdam could in fact amount to over nine per cent.[30]

When possible therefore, the larger specialist exporters would attempt to circumvent the Dutch granaries both for export and import, and the official statistics indicate that, as far as exports of bread grains were concerned, they were largely successful in doing so during the 1720s and 1730s.[31] But a certain proportion of the trade in English bread grains was handled by the Dutch both as agents acting for English principals and as merchants exporting on their own accounts. The Rotterdam notarial archives contain numerous instances of Rotterdam merchants chartering English vessels lying in that port for grain voyages usually sailing in ballast but sometimes with mixed cargoes from Rotterdam to an English port to load a cargo of wheat, and then back to Rotterdam or on to a European port for disposal of the grain. Some of these voyages were doubtless made on the instructions of English principals: Ralph Carr's Dutch agent T. M. Liebenrood, for example, is frequently named in the agreements.[32] But others were clearly undertaken by Dutch merchants on their own accounts such as those of William Konink exporting English coal and grain to Norway and returning to Holland with timber, or J. P. Charron, who regularly imported their own grain from England and were quick to complain of its quality. The most frequently recurring name is that of the famous Rotterdam house, Archibald and Isaac Hope trading in wheat and barley to Southern Europe.[33]

At the same time the Hopes were deeply involved in the Anglo-Dutch malt trade, and the will of Archibald Hope Sr, dated 1720, shows him to have been the owner of malting houses in Ipswich, Stowmarket, and Bury St Edmunds and of two vessels used specially for the transport of malt.[34] It seems therefore that Dutch capital played an important part in the English grain export trade though the precise amount cannot be specified. Some contemporaries alleged that French capital was employed in the trade, with English exporters contracting to deliver wheat at fixed prices to French importers but the evidence here is less reliable.[35] It is not clear whether bounty payments were actually received by foreign importers though in 1714 we find the Maisters, as agents for London merchants, collecting bounty money in Hull and remitting the proceeds to London.[36] Presumably such remittances could equally well be sent abroad or balanced against freight charges and commission.

This brief survey indicates that disposal of the English grain surplus became a highly commercialised activity during the first half of the eighteenth century, with a marked degree of specialisation between the two groups of grains, the 'industrial' grains, malt and barley, and the bread grains, wheat, rye and oatmeal. The state of overseas demand and a range of commercial imperatives, including the availability of shipping space, commercial intelligence and the level of Baltic supplies were no less important than the state of the home market in determining whether grain would be exported or retained for home consumption, particularly that of the metropolis. The momentum behind the trade was largely generated by the merchant, while its rationale was provided by the temporary convergence of landed and mercantile interests.

IV Agrarian Improvement and English Competitiveness

We must now consider England's competitive position in the international grain trade, particularly in relation to that of its closest rivals, the Dutch. As early as 1711 Davenant had concluded with satisfaction that 'in this branch of trade, we have in a great measure supplanted those northern countries from whence Holland was heretofore furnished with grain'[1] and it is true that the period of bulk export from England coincided very closely with one of prolonged decline in the largely Dutch-controlled Baltic grain trade (*c.* 1690–1760). There is no need to emphasise here the immense importance which the Baltic grain trade held for a number of key sectors in the Dutch economy, nor to recapitulate Professor Faber's well-known account of its decline.[2] We may however agree with M. Morineau that Faber did not sufficiently underline the importance of English grain in making good the continuing shortfall caused by declining Baltic shipments.[3] Professor John took this argument a stage further by suggesting that a high rate of agrarian improvement together with an extension of the cultivated area were responsible for the 'highly competitive' position of English grain during the first sixty years of the eighteenth century, and particularly between the early 1730s and 1750; this cost advantage, he argued, bolstered up by subsidies, produced a situation in which English grain was displacing Baltic grain in European markets.[4] The likely extent of these supply changes is indicated in the figures assembled in Table 5, overleaf.

It is clear that total English grain exports were comparable in magnitude to shipments through the Sound from the very early years of the century, and greatly exceeded the latter during the period 1730 to 1760. But it must be remembered that the greater proportion of Baltic grain cargoes consisted of wheat and rye, with

Table 5: Grain Shipments through the Sound, compared with English Grain Exports, 1680–9 to 1760–9, Decennial Averages, '000 quarters

	Grain shipments through the Sound[1]	English exports of wheat, rye and oatmeal[2]	English exports of malt and barley
1680–89	905.1		
(1685–86)		17.4	1.0
1690–99	587.2	3.9	46.8
1700–09	316.1	153.8	128.7
1710–19	283.7	137.2	231.5
1720–29	431.9	129.7	286.1
1730–39	336.4	312.9	221.4
1740–49	337.2	361.2	304.6
1750–59	393.0	372.2	285.2
1760–69	587.6	259.1	187.0

[1] Shipments through the Sound have been converted into quarters on the basis 1 Dutch Last = 10.75 Imperial Quarters. From data kindly supplied by Prof. J.A. Faber on which was based his graph B, 'Decline of Baltic Grain Trade', loc. cit., p. 117. In reading these figures, it should be remembered that the proportion of the Baltic grain trade handled by the Dutch remained fairly constant at 70 to 80 per cent until the 1720s from which point the proportion fell continually to about 50 per cent by the 1780s (see below pp. 65–6).

[2] English exports = gross exports throughout. No account is taken of the substantial wheat imports of the years 1765 to 1769.

malt and barley occupying a fluctuating but usually minor position in the trade. In 1667, a year for which information is readily available, malt and barley accounted for as much as one-third of Amsterdam's grain imports; in 1692, the figure was one-seventh.[5] While English exports of malt and barley replaced these Baltic imports in some degree, the massive trade in these grains from East Anglian ports in the eighteenth century was largely opening up a new area of demand in Holland – that of the distiller.[6] Bearing this in mind then, it is apparent that English exports of bread grains only began to 'displace' Baltic shipments on a substantial scale during the period *c.*, 1730 to 1760. Furthermore there is a clear interval from the 1680s, when Baltic shipments begin to decline, to the year 1703 when English exports begin to increase.[7]

It seems therefore that there is no immediate chronological connection between the decline of the Baltic grain trade and the growth of English exports. Throughout this period of course, international grain movements were extremely marginal to the food requirements of Europe as a whole, and Faber's suggestion of a slight downturn in the demand for Baltic grain in the later seventeenth and early eighteenth centuries is a plausible explanation for the sustained decline of these years. Stagnation of population, together with increasing self-sufficiency in grain production in certain parts of western and southern Europe were, according to Faber, the major determinants of this reduced demand.[8] France, Germany, and the southern Netherlands, especially Brabant, began to produce sizable surpluses from the later seventeenth century, and de Vries has recently pointed to a revival of domestic grain production in Holland in the 1690s. Zeeland in the south-west and Groningen in the north-east began sending regular shipments to the traditional grain deficit areas and to the cities.[9]

These changes not only reduced the demand for Baltic grain for international redistribution from Amsterdam but also made the Dutch themselves less dependent upon Baltic supplies. (During the second half of the seventeenth century, over half Amsterdam's grain imports were on average retained for domestic consumption).[10] At the same time, it seems that supply conditions in Eastern Europe were beginning to alter. Wyczański has shown that productivity (as measured by the level of the harvest) was declining in some areas of Poland between 1660 and 1765 due to soil exhaustion, the fragmentation of peasant holdings and loss of population.[11] To falling yields should be added the widespread devastation caused by the Great Northern War of 1700 to 1721, which coincided with a particularly severe outbreak of plague from 1706 to 1713. The survey of Polish crown lands undertaken from 1710 to 1715 constantly reported heavy losses of population, destruction of buildings, untilled fields, absence of estate inventories, and lack of corn for sowing. In parts of Lithuania and Western Galicia, up to 90 per cent of farms had been deserted.[12] It is likely therefore that the tailing-off of Baltic grain supplies was largely independent of England's entry into the European grain trade until perhaps the 1730s, although English exporters doubtless took advantage of the situation. Davenant realised much of this when he wrote in 1711, 'corn is in a manner a new exportation arising to us from the war, which has in other countries so employed the hands of their people that they could not till the ground; or from deaths or plagues, wherewith divers nations have been afflicted for these last 23 years.'[13]

From about 1730 onwards however, European demand for cereals revived. After a long period of stagnation, population began to increase, especially in southern Europe. The most dramatic growth occurred in Spain's population which increased by one-third over a forty-year period: from seven millions in 1712–17 to 9.3 millions in 1756–8,[14] while that of Portugal increased from 2.1 to 2.5 millions between 1732 and 1770.[15] Significant increases also occurred in France and some of the Italian states.[16] Although the population of Holland was declining during this period,[17] Dutch demand for overseas bread grains increased during the 1740s when Brabant was no longer in a position to export its surplus rye and buckwheat.[18] The shortages of these years were doubtless exacerbated by the high prices and scarcity of meat and dairy products which followed the prolonged outbreak of cattle plague in the Netherlands from 1744 – one of the most serious aspects of what van der Woude has called a 'crisis situation' in the agriculture of North Holland.[19] The late 1740s and early 1750s were marked by dearth in both France and Holland. In 1747, mobs plundered grain vessels at Rotterdam and Brielle, the cargoes of which were destined for France, though the most serious shortages occurred from 1749 to 1751.[20]

In broad outline therefore, it seems that a variety of somewhat adventitious circumstances provided English farmers with exceptionally favourable overseas market opportunities in the first half of the eighteenth century. During the initial phase of export prior to *c.* 1732, changes on the supply side predominated with the dislocation of East European agriculture and the trade of the Baltic ports, while European demand remained moderate. The demand for malt and barley however was much more elastic than that for bread grains and, given the fiscal advantages attached to this branch of trade, its expansion is not surprising. In the second phase of export from *c.* 1732 demand for bread grains in Europe increased substantially and English producers, experiencing a run of exceptionally favourable seasons, were able to respond. In these circumstances, the role played by agricultural improvement may be less significant than Professor John argued, and the suggestion that 'grain exports might be regarded in a very approximate way as the measurement of investment in agriculture' in the improved areas, must be viewed with scepticism.[21]

How competitive in fact was English agriculture during the first half of the eighteenth century? It is now widely accepted that for much of the period 1650 to 1750, agriculture in many parts of Europe was in a depressed condition, characterised by a low and falling level of grain prices. Although the complaints of farmers and landlords sometimes give a contrary impression, the extent of the price fall in England's case was only moderate and, perhaps more important, the absolute level of English cereal prices was high by European standards from the late seventeenth century onwards. The cereal price index constructed by Abel illustrates the first of these points: taking the first half of the period (1650–1700) as a base of 100, the index falls in the second half century (1701–50) to 84 for England, 75 for France, 73 for the Southern Netherlands, 70 for the United Provinces, and 60 for Poland. In the case of Germany and Austria, the index rises (104 and 103 respectively), and for Denmark and Northern Italy, it shows a moderate fall to 90 in each case.[22] On the second point, relating to the absolute level of English grain prices, Braudel and Spooner have shown beyond reasonable doubt that English wheat, measured in silver prices, was the most expensive in Europe during most of the years from 1690 to 1760, (the 1740s being an exception).[23] This is hardly surprising when we consider the nature of the unique agrarian structure which was developing in England during the early modern period, and especially after the Civil War: one of large estates divided into compact tenanted farms, highly capitalised, and worked by free wage labour. The contrast with the more labour-intensive peasant farming of France and Spain, or the serf agriculture of Eastern Europe, is obvious enough, and the differences were reflected in relative price levels.

Exact comparison of international wheat prices is extremely difficult for the eighteenth century, when qualitative differences were rarely specified, but some indication of the competitive position of English wheat in relation to East European supplies may be obtained from the material assembled in Table 6. London (Bear Quay) prices are substantially lower than any other recorded English series, including Dover, yet remain well above Danzig prices throughout the period, except for the 1740s. The only means therefore by which English grain could compete with Baltic grain in European markets were through either lower transfer cost or a more advantageous timing of despatch. It is certain that the English grain trade was fairly active during the winter months when the Baltic ports were frozen up. Ralph Carr, for example, sometimes asked his correspondents for information on grain prices 'in the spring, before the Baltic is open.'[24] But it was mainly through lower transfer costs that English merchants were able to compete with Dutch suppliers of Baltic grain who faced the additional expense of transhipment via Amsterdam. Voyages from London and the east coast ports to Southern Europe were obviously shorter and cheaper than those from Danzig and Kongisberg and above all, English exporters enjoyed the advantage of the bounty which they often regarded as covering handling and freight charges. In 1738, Carr wrote to his Dunkirk agent 'I could have any quantity [of barley] at 14s p. qr. besides getting the bounty [of 2s 6d] which wd. pay a great part of the fraught and other charges'.[25] At that time, the Maisters were chartering vessels to carry wheat to Cadiz at 4s per quarter which, together with handling and port charges, was exactly covered by 5s bounty.[26] It is abundantly clear that without the benefit of the bounty to absorb transfer costs, English grain would not have found a market in Europe – and in this sense, Adam Smith and others were correct in referring to the corn trade as a 'forced export'.[27] To the extent that the 'competitiveness' of English grain

Table 6: European Wheat Prices, 1700s–1750s
Decennial averages, shillings per quarter

	Eton	Dover	London	Amsterdam	Dordt	Polish Wheat, A'dam Bourse	Konigsberg Wheat A'dam Bourse	Danzig
1700–09	36.07	44.10	29.58	–	37.69*	34.71*	29.77*	21.90
1710–19	44.89	39.01	38.11	29.05	35.50	–	–	26.47
1720–29	38.45	37.32	32.68	28.22	28.78	–	–	20.23
1730–39	32.78	31.60	27.86	26.26	26.48	26.63*	22.28*	19.48
1740–49	32.61	32.78	27.71	33.62	33.98	36.62*	30.75*	24.23
1750–59	38.50	37.74	32.74	30.80	32.73	29.52*	27.74*	22.91

Sources:

Eton, Dordt, Danzig   J. Marshall, *A Digest of All the Accounts* (1833) pp. 98–9.
Amsterdam   BPP, 1826–7 (Consuls' Returns).
Dover   D. A. Baker, 'The Agriculture of Kent, 1660–1760' (University of Kent Ph.D. thesis, 1976).
London   M. Combrune, *Enquiry into the Prices of Wheat, Malt, &c* (1768) p. 74.
Amsterdam Bourse   N. W. Posthumus, *Nederlandsche Prijsgeschiedenis*, I (1943) pp. 2–6.

* fewer than ten quotations available

depended upon artificial rather than cost advantages, we might suppose that improvements in productivity played a limited part in this process.

Contemporary supporters as well as critics of the bounty system recognised that the existence of bounties was essential to the continuation of the export trade, though only the latter accepted that the subsidy tended to raise prices above their 'natural' level in both the long and the short run. The weight of evidence suggests that bounties did in fact tend to raise grain prices, for reasons which have been elaborated by a long line of writers following Adam Smith, which includes Alfred Marshall, C. R. Fay, and T. S. Ashton.[28] Only if the most plausible assumptions about eighteenth-century agriculture were abandoned – that the demand for bread grains was fairly inelastic and that industry was subject to diminishing returns – could we conclude (as the supporters of the bounty did) that its long-term effects were to increase the area of arable cultivation and lower the prices of wheat and other bread grains. It seems likely, therefore, that the growth of a subsidised export trade partly explains why English grain prices did not sink to the disastrously low levels found in certain parts of Europe during the eighteenth century.[29] And it is significant that during the second phase of export, when English grain came to dominate European markets, the trend of Amsterdam prices rose to reach the higher English levels, suggesting that it was the increasing scale of European demand, rather than English 'competitiveness' which attracted English grain to Europe in increased quantities.(Figure 4).

If increasing agricultural productivity did not supply the essential momentum behind the expansion of the trade, then what did? And how was the surplus for export generated? In fact the early history of bounty policy suggests that a substantial surplus for export *already* existed in the 1670s; indeed one of the aims of that policy was to reduce the 'redundancy' of corn which was depressing farmers' incomes.[30] 'From the time the bounty on corn exports went into force in 1674 or 1675 up to about 1680,' wrote N.S.B. Gras, 'the increase in exports is striking'. On the basis of statistics of bounty debentures, Gras estimated the total annual average export of grain at 303,925 quarters for the years 1675 to 1677, which com-

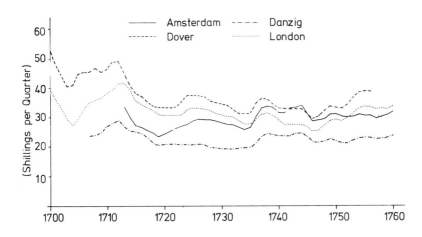

Figure 4: European Wheat Prices, 1700–60 (nine year moving averages)
Sources: See Table 6, note on sources

pares with the known figure of 353,353 quarters in the period 1697 to 1731.[31] To some extent, merchants may have been withdrawing grain from the home market for sale overseas, as is suggested by a number of provincial correspondents whose letters survive amongst the State Papers. A report from Falmouth of 1675 reads 'Much corn is buying up in those parts for the Canaries and Holland, so that the price is raised since harvest 3s on twenty gallons and is like to be dearer, for the encouragement the merchant has of 5s per quarter paid them at the custom house very much encourages them to buy; so that the act which is good for the farmers, is not beneficial to the town.'[32] The poor people he added, 'begin to murmur'.[33] In the following year, a correspondent from Bridlington reported that 'some wheat is shipped here and gone for Holland, and much more will be exported if the Act continue(s) unrepealed . . . . Corn is already a considerable price for the encouragement of husbandry, but, if this Act be continued, it will advance much more, and take much from the revenue and be very hard for the poor.'[34]

Certainly, the decline in exports which followed the lapse of the bounty in 1681 is very striking, and the results of this 'experimental period' during the 1670s seem to suggest that earlier improvements in farming methods had generated a sizable surplus for export, which might be supplemented by withdrawals from domestic consumption. At no time during the entire period did grain exports constitute more than a small fraction of total output, averaging only 3 per cent during the first half of the eighteenth century, and 6.8 per cent in the peak year of 1750.[35] The increase in production and/or productivity needed to achieve the export surplus was thus relatively small, and lay within the capabilities of late seventeenth-century farmers. Several agricultural historians now associate the middle and later decades of the seventeenth century with a breakthrough in the adoption of new crops and farming methods, including E. L. Jones who has seen this early rise in agricultural productivity as one which 'permitted a large growth of London's population and led to an expansion of grain exports'.[36]

This is not the place for detailed comments on this literature, and much still remains to be discovered about the chronology of innovation during the early modern period. A recent attempt to estimate the pace of root crop innovation in East Anglia from the late sixteenth to the early eighteenth centuries indicates that the half century following the Restoration was indeed a critical period. M. Overton's results, obtained from probate inventories, show a rapid and sustained increase in the use of root crops from the 1660s up to 1715, followed by a slight downturn until 1735 when the data end.[37] But the influence of turnips and clover as indicators of agricultural progress has probably been exaggerated, and neither were associated with any clear rise in crop yields before the later eighteenth century. Overton comments:[38]

> When the farming environment began to change dramatically after the mid-eighteenth century, farmers were well prepared to respond to increasing demand with turnips and clover established within their farming systems. If we trace the development of production changes *ex ante* rather than *ex post*, then agricultural development seems a much less certain process. While the changes of *c.* 1650 to *c.* 1750 had vital

consequences they were probably both unforeseen and unintended. The paths to progress then . . . were circuitous rather than direct.

The evidence relating to crop yields is even more ambiguous, and has been summarised by M. Turner who provides some reliable national estimates for the 1790s, from which a mean output per acre for wheat of 19.5 bushels can be derived.[39] B. Holderness estimates wheat yields in the range 12–28 bushels per acre (modal output 18 bushels) for the period 1650 to 1690, based on national trends,[40] while Overton's results for East Anglia suggest wheat yields of 14–16 bushels per acre for the late seventeenth century.[41] Overton's data end in 1735 and reliable estimates for the remainder of the eighteenth century are lacking. Depending upon one's selection of estimates, increases of between 10 and 40 per cent can be suggested for the eighteenth century, but the precise level and chronology of change has yet to be determined. The most un-ambiguous evidence, that for East Anglia, suggests that the most notable gains in productivity occurred between the 1590s and the 1670s for wheat, barley and oats, with a short spurt of improvement from *c.* 1700 to 1715. Gains of at least 75 per cent are recorded for this earlier period, and Kerridge's statement that an early agricultural revolution was largely complete by 1673 finds verification in improvements of this order.[42]

As far as the increased growth of cereal exports is concerned in the period after 1732, there is some reason to think that population stagnation from *c.* 1720 to 1745 released food resources for export. Estimated population totals for England and Wales produced by the Cambridge Group for the History of Population and Social Structure indicate a higher rate of growth of population during the first two decades of the eighteenth century than earlier estimates, and place the demographic recession firmly in the 1720s rather than the 1700s where Rickman had located it.[43] While stagnation of population may not have been a nation-wide phenomenon after 1720, Chambers concluded that 'for the Midlands and the Home Counties, for Manchester, Liverpool and Birmingham, and above all London . . . there can be no doubt about it.'[44] A variety of epidemic attacks were probably responsible – typhus, smallpox, and enteric fevers, and in London's case, already high death rates were increased by the effects of gin drinking. After 1730, new building in London virtually ceased.[45] London parishes are excluded from the Cambridge Group's aggregative sample of 404 parishes, but Wrigley and Schofield have applied a series of correctives to the evidence contained in the bills of mortality. Expressed as decadal totals, this shows a marked rise in burials between the second and third decades of the eighteenth century while baptisms rise less sharply, supporting the view of near-contemporaries such as Corbyn Morris that the 1720s were conspicuous as an excessively unhealthy period in London's history.[46] A major consequence of this 'calamitous setback'[47] to the metropolitan population must have been a reduced demand for foodstuffs, particularly coastal imports of grain. Since the early part of the sixteenth century, a growing number of English farmers had directed their efforts towards producing larger surpluses for the London wholesalers, and the tendency was for localised markets to yield increasingly to metropolitan influence. Gras and later Fisher, explained how a network of grain-importing middlemen developed, to establish these developing channels of supply.[48] From the later seventeenth century onwards however, a new pattern emerges; a small proportion of the surplus grain which was previously sent to London for the consumption of its inhabitants was instead directed overseas. We have already noticed how the export trade in bread grains was organised to a large extent from London, and how a large proportion of the trade was carried on London merchants' accounts – larger than the export statistics alone would indicate.[49] It seems plausible to suggest, therefore, that during the 'demographic retreat' of the period 1720 to 1745 a somewhat enlarged grain surplus was being diverted overseas by London merchants and corn factors at a time when metropolitan demand was relatively stagnant.

A second set of circumstances which tended to enlarge the volume of grain shipments after *c.* 1732 was, of course, good weather combined with the effects of the agricultural depression of the years 1730 to 1750.[50] It is well known that the thirties and forties saw an exceptional run of favourable seasons and good harvests. A succession of good harvests enhanced the supply of grain, Chambers noted 'while a series of epidemics was thinning the ranks of those who could have consumed it.'[51] Thomas Tooke commented: 'from 1730 to 1739, both years included, there does not appear to have been one season with any general or marked deficiency.'[52] The forties were even better. From 1741 to 1751 wrote Sir Charles Smith, 'we had ten as good years as ever were known in succession.'[53] Tooke in fact accepted and elaborated Adam Smith's earlier argument that the 'accidental variation of the seasons' was the crucial factor explaining the contrasting price history of the twenty years preceding 1750 and the twenty preceding 1770.[54] There is now little doubt that the low prices of the thirties and forties brought about widespread agricultural depression and in explaining how the supply of foodstuffs temporarily outstripped demand, Professor Mingay concluded (like Smith and Tooke) that 'the key factor in the situation was almost certainly the unusually long succession of good harvests.'[55] Wheat was more sensitive than any other cereal to variations in weather conditions and a prolonged run of good seasons could result in a dramatic increase in output. The extent of such increases was often exaggerated by contemporaries. Sir James Steuart believed it was commonly held that an abundant crop provided more than three years' subsistence.[56] Josiah Tucker suggested as much as five years.[57] Steuart himself considered the surplus in an 'ordinary good year' to be equivalent to fourteen months' full subsistence; in an exceptional year, no more than fifteen months'.[58] In other words a good harvest could increase the supply of grain by perhaps 16 per cent (equal to 2¼ million quarters in the 1730s), or at most by 25 per cent. Whatever the precise figure might be, the essential point to note is that a well-informed contemporary believed that a substantial surplus could be generated by a run of good seasons, of an order which clearly exceeded the peak levels of export of the period 1748 to 1752.

It is clear from their correspondence that exporting merchants were quick to take advantage of the difficulties facing farmers during these years of plenty and low prices. 'Wheat comes just now plenty to market', wrote Ralph Carr in November 1738 'which is owing to the poverty of the farmers who want money very much, yet am of opinion stocks will fall so much short in the spring, therefore am determined to continue buying all the good parcels I can meet with.'[59] The Lancaster trader William Stout explained how low grain prices in 1733 'went hard with poor farmers, and broke many, and lessened the rent of land' but contrasted the situation facing farmers in the north-west with that in southern England from whence, he noted, great quantities of corn were exported to France, Spain, and Italy 'which was a great relief to the farmers.'[60] Expectation of changes in the weather often determined decisions whether to export or build up stocks: 'prices of wheat are but very midling so that I ordered mine to be laid up; at the time of my finding it every one were glad to get their quantity of corn off at any rate as we had then a prospect of a most plentiful harvest, indeed our wheat was well got in.'[61]

We must conclude, therefore, that farmers in the arable regions were supplying the export trade as a means of alleviating their distress during the depressed years of the thirties and forties,[62] in which case the level of exports might be regarded as a measure of their difficulties rather than an indicator of the buoyancy of the agricultural sector. Indeed, this is the reason why the bounty was so vigorously defended in the early 1750s when the first serious attacks upon it were mounted. 'Without the bounty', it was said in 1752, 'no corn will be exported; and . . . without an exportation [the farmer] could not pay his rent.'[63] To the extent that exports alleviated farmers' difficulties during these years, they must have tended to raise prices, and this is one reason why grain riots occurred during this period and not always in times of acute shortage. On May 12 1737, for example, a Salisbury newspaper reported:[64]

> A load of wheat belonging to Farmer Waters, of Burford, going to Redbridge for exportation was stopped near Whiteparish by about 60 people, who knocked down the fore horse, broke the wagon in pieces, cut the sacks and strewed about the corn. They threatened to do the like to all who sold wheat for exportation.

As E. P. Thompson has emphasised, eighteenth-century food riots cannot be 'explained' in terms of spasmodic hunger and harvest failure alone: grievances were felt when the popular consensus as to the legitimacy of various marketing practices appeared to have been broken.[65] And the operation of the Corn Laws provided little safeguard to the consumer against what might be termed 'unsocial export'. In good years, the bounty tended to send the entire surplus overseas, so that in a bad year, substantial import was necessary as if the bounty had not existed.[66] To the merchant of course, the import trade was equally, if not more profitable, than the export trade. Furthermore in poor harvest years, withdrawal of the bounty often occurred too late to prevent dearth, as in 1740 when in Yarmouth itself, scarcity was such that a mob rose and plundered a vessel about to clear overseas with a cargo of wheat. The rioters compelled corn dealers to sell at two shillings per bushel until order was finally restored by a company of dragoons from Norwich.[67] Defoe summarised a commonly-held view when he agreed that the bounty tended to raise artificially the price of corn, and 'though it may be a damage to some particular persons, and may pinch the poor, who yet for ought I see, are always alike poor, in plenty as in scarcity.'[68]

Professor John argued – as one commentator has pointed out, with an element of circularity – that the relationship between grain exports and improved farming was reciprocal: that is to say, agricultural improvement provided the basis from which the export trade developed in the first instance, and the continued existence of the trade itself acted as a major stimulus to the steady growth of productivity thereafter.[69] The evidence in fact suggests that the relationship may have been more simple: that seventeenth-century farming improvements certainly provided the basis for England's entry into the international grain trade, but that the continued growth of this branch of trade probably depended upon factors other than agrarian improvement. Grain exports, in particular, cannot be safely used as a measure of eighteenth-century agricultural productivity, especially during the depression of the period 1730 to 1750. Significantly, this view is very close to that suggested by Skene Keith (which was outlined in chapter one) and which associated improved farming with the later rather than the earlier part of the eighteenth century.[70] The notion that increased productivity followed from grain exports was one which was first developed, largely as a polemic, by the supporters of the export bounty when that legislation came under serious attack from the 1750s onwards,[71] and it has since been uncritically accepted by a number of modern historians (though Fay and Ashton were exceptions). In fact the supporters of the bounty system greatly enlarged the single connection which perhaps did exist between improved farming and grain exports; namely, the extension of barley cultivation in rotation.[72] Because the demand of home and overseas brewers and distillers was fairly elastic in the period under consideration, a larger area of land under barley would result in increased farm income and at the same time form part of mixed farming systems which provided the best safeguard against falling grain prices.[73] This specific aspect of Norfolk farming can legitimately be linked with the encouragement of the bounty, but it was made at the cost of possibly substantial abuses in the malt trade.

V Grain Exports and the Dutch Economy

While it may be incorrect to suggest that English grain exports actually undermined the Dutch-controlled Baltic trade, there is little doubt that English exporters profited from the variety of circumstances described in the previous chapter which caused Baltic grain shipments to stagnate from the late seventeenth century. It is important, however, to avoid the errors of those contemporaries who suggested that a profitable trade must necessarily be driven at the expense of competitors. Professor John's assertions that English grain exports damaged the Dutch economy and that 'Holland's loss was England's gain' are misleading in several respects.[1] The advantages enjoyed by English landowners and farmers in the form of higher prices were obtained at the expense of domestic consumers rather than that of the Dutch, whose economic well-being depended on a steady supply of imported grain to supplement home production.

It is clear that the shift in European demand from Baltic to English sources did indeed reduce the derived demand for Dutch shipping in this important branch of trade. But on balance, it is probable that the Dutch economy benefitted from the import of subsidised English grain. We have already seen that England's entry into the international grain trade was facilitated if not actually brought into being by the dislocation of Baltic supplies – so that in reality, English grain shipments provided the only alternative to shortages and higher prices.[2] Shipping from the Baltic to Holland suffered not only during the Great Northern War of the years 1700 to 1721 but also as a result of the Nine Years' War and the War of the Spanish Succession. In each successive decade from 1688 to 1721, Baltic shipping to Holland declined by about one-third. When peace was restored in 1721, Dutch-Baltic shipping recovered to such an extent as to exceed the previous high level of the 1680s.[3] With the outbreak of the War of the Polish Succession in 1731 however, Dutch-Baltic trade was again dislocated for several years. In 1734, William Stout explained that great quantities of grain were being shipped from London and Southern England, 'there being now heavy wars in Poland upon the election of a King; Dantzig besieged, and much destroyed, from whence most of Europe was supplied with corn; and now the country is so ruined that they fear a famine there, as also in Germany.'[4]

Without these substantial grain shipments from England to make good the continuing shortfall of imports from the Baltic, Holland's domestic economy as well as her international trading position would have faced added strains. Wages in the Dutch Republic were already higher than those of its competitors, and high food prices would have widened the gap still further.[5] With a small and specialised agricultural sector and a substantial industrial base, which remained tied to overseas markets, the Dutch were extremely vulnerable to increases in the price of imported grain. De Vries has shown how the functioning of the entire Dutch economy depended upon its ability to obtain regular supplies of overseas grain: by the mid-seventeenth century, foreign grain fed well over half the million inhabitants of Holland, Utrecht, Friesland and Groningen, and the position changed little over the next century.[6] Over a long period, the Dutch had freed themselves from the necessity for extensive arable cultivation which enabled them to devote resources to more productive activities. The labour and capital thus released found employment in industry and commerce, and a highly specialised form of agriculture developed on the basis of dairying and the production of industrial crops.[7] Only when harvests failed over large areas of Europe did Dutch farmers temporarily revert to a more balanced system of mixed farming, as in 1709, when a Rotterdam correspondent reported that 'At present, corn being so dear, it is the opinion of most people that instead of sowing flax, the country people will sow corn.' The price of rapeseed, he added, would probably rise for the same reason.[8]

The nature and extent of food crises in the pre-industrial Netherlands has recently been surveyed by Professor Faber, who concluded that, in the seventeenth and eighteenth centuries, scarcity was less severe and price rises less extreme than in most other European countries.[9] The favourable situation, he observes, is to be explained by Holland's position at the centre of the world market for grain, together with a relatively high level of real wages which implies a higher elasticity of demand for grain than was the case elsewhere.[10] Although Faber insisted that these conclusions were based on impressionistic evidence, the relatively moderate extent of fluctuations in the price of wheat in Holland as compared with other parts of Europe is borne out by the evidence assembled in figure 5. Price fluctuations on the Amsterdam market seem to have been less marked than those displayed by the London market from 1713 to 1760, with the exception of 1740/1. On the other hand, the instability of French grain markets (against which Faber compared the position of Holland) seems to have been somewhat exceptional in the eighteenth century.[11] Nevertheless, the relatively small size of the United Provinces and its population together with the excellence of internal communications meant that dearth in any part of the country could easily be relieved in all but the most severe years of shortage.[12] The granaries of Amsterdam seldom held less than 200,000 quarters of grain,[13] and during years of scarcity, overseas export was prohibited by the States General.[14] Although the level of duties on imported grain was frequently disputed amongst the Admiralty Colleges, with those of Zeeland and Friesland demanding stronger protection for their own agriculture, the opposition of the Admiralties of Holland prevailed, and duties remained low.[15] The tariff reforms of 1681 and 1725 abolished export duties on grain, and import duties on wheat and rye amounted to no more than 3 or 4 per cent of real values.[16]

Although figures are not available to indicate the quantity of grain imports retained for domestic consumption, the course of prices suggests that the Dutch were successful in maintaining an adequate supply of imported grain which, given the specialised nature of Dutch agriculture, was essential to feed a relatively large urban population. By subsidising the export of surplus grain to Holland and other markets, English landlords were passing on the advantages of low food prices at a time when alternative supplies from the Baltic were interrupted. As consumers of imported grain, the Dutch could hardly fail to benefit from this situation;[17] but as merchants and carriers of grain, it is likely that the Dutch suffered from English competition in this extremely important branch of trade, which in the seventeenth century had provided the basis for Amsterdam's prosperity. To what extent was this the case?

From time to time, Dutch corn merchants did indeed complain of English competition in the international grain trade. In the discussions preceding the *Propositie* of 1751, when the Admiralties of Holland came into conflict on the question of grain import duties, the Maas College argued for the total abolition of import duties on wheat, rye, and barley, on the grounds that English merchants were underselling the Dutch in Mediterranean markets.[18] The Amsterdammers however, anxious to maintain their income from the existing duties, put forward a more confident position, arguing that the trade could easily bear a low duty and that their long credit was indispensable.[19] Earlier in the century, Davenant had warned that the Dutch were pressing for high duties on imported English grain, especially malt, in retaliation against the English duty increases on Dutch linens.[20] But these complaints were made by specific interest groups arguing particular cases; they did not represent English competition as an urgent threat and in fact they were not acted upon.

The impact of English competition in the carrying trade was modified by two sets of circumstances. In the first place, we have already noticed that a certain amount of Dutch capital and shipping was in any case employed in the English grain trade. Dutch agents were frequently used by English exporters and Dutch merchants are known to have exported English grain on their own accounts; and it seems that some Dutch capital was employed in the East Anglian malt trade.[21] Recourse was made to Dutch and other foreign shipping during wartime and when the flow of grain exports was reversed, as in 1728, 1740, and the later 1760s, shortages were relieved by wheat and rye imported from Dutch ports in Dutch ships.[22] Early in the century, Davenant had complained that 'in years of scarcity, they [the Dutch] bring us back our own wheat, because of the premium we give upon exportation, and which they are enabled to do, by having large granaries almost in every great town'.[23]

In the second place, it appears that Dutch merchant capital found more profitable employment in trades other than the carriage of Baltic grain, given that the domestic market was now adequately supplied with English grain. A number of writers have drawn attention to the fact that activity in the Dutch-Baltic grain trade corresponded closely to the level of grain prices prevailing in Danzig and Amsterdam, with falling prices producing stagnation or decline. This relationship seems to apply in the case of secular trends as well as short term movements; thus, van Dillen accounted for the decline of the period 1650 to 1680, the revival of the 1680s and 90s, and the stagnation of the period 1720 to 1750 by reference to low grain prices, while Dr Knoppers had explained annual Dutch-Baltic shipping movements in similar terms during the first half of the eighteenth century.[24] Certainly, contemporaries were well aware of this. 'The importation of foreign corn [is] very considerable;' wrote the English agent in Rotterdam, 'this is all laid upon store which is a sign that the Dutch, who understand this trade as well as any nation whatsoever, expect that there will be a great demand from abroad.'[25]

During the first half of the eighteenth century therefore, and especially in the period 1720 to 1750, it is not surprising that the Baltic grain trade stagnated when a period of low grain prices coincided with several other restraining influences, notably, political disturbances and disruption of trade, increasing self sufficiency in grain production in Southern and Western Europe, and a growing preference for wheat in place of rye, which implied a shift away from Baltic suppliers. But not only did the Baltic grain trade as a whole stagnate – there was an absolute and relative decline in the share of that trade handled by the Dutch in the period 1721 to 1780, as compared with the period 1661 to 1720. During the earlier of these two periods, the Dutch handled over 80 per cent of the rye and nearly 90 per cent of the wheat transported through the Sound, whereas the proportion fell continually in the decade after 1720 to reach 55 per cent for rye and 49 per cent for wheat in the 1780s.[26] A larger share of the trade was now being handled by Scandinavians and Hansards. By itself, this substantial decline in Dutch-Baltic grain shipments would have proved extremely damaging to the Dutch economy; but in fact it seems that Dutch merchants were merely shifting their interests from grain to other products. On these 'compensatory movements' within Dutch-Baltic trade, in the period 1720 to 1750, van Dillen has written:[27]

> New Baltic trades grew to replace the old ones. The decline of the grain trade was matched by a decline in the shipment of the traditional outward cargoes, herrings and salt. But compensation for this was provided by an enormous expansion of imports of timber from the Baltic area and of exports of textiles and colonial wares to it. The imports of timber from the Baltic, mainly oak, but also pine from the forests of Livonia and Estonia, grew at a truly astonishing rate. From the decade 1661–70, when imports amounted to no more than about one million 'pieces', the supply of timber grew to almost five million in 1721–30 and reached an ample ten million pieces in the next decade, a high level which was more or less retained until 1780.

While the English and the Swedes participated in the rapid expansion of the Baltic timber trade which occurred after 1720, the Dutch retained the lion's share throughout the period. The great upsurge in the export of colonial goods to the Baltic also occurred after 1720, and although the Swedes, the Danes and the Hansards succeeded in increasing their share of this trade at the expense of the Dutch and the English, that of the last two nevertheless showed substantial absolute increases.[28] It is largely because of these adjustments within the structure of Dutch-Baltic trade that the number of ships that sailed from the Baltic to Holland more than doubled between 1710 and 1719 and 1750 and 1759 in spite of the tailing-off of grain shipments.[29]

Around 1760 however, Baltic grain prices began to rise and the Baltic grain trade revived just as the period of massive English grain exports was drawing to a close.[30] The most substantial demands to be placed on Amsterdam's granaries during these years came from the growing markets of France and the Southern Netherlands.[31] At the same time, with the rising level of cereal prices, the earlier protracted depression of Dutch farming came to an end. Against these improvements in the economic situation however, must be set the detrimental consequences of higher food prices, especially in so far as these affected the level of internal purchasing power. Faber has suggested that the cost of living began to rise as early as 1740, but points out that the discrepancy between rising prices and the stationary level of wages became substantial only after *c.* 1770.[32] Nevertheless, it is clear that from about mid-century, the fortunes of Dutch industry and agriculture began to diverge considerably and if, as one historian has alleged, the rural background to the political upheavals of the later eighteenth century was one of steadily accumulating well-being,[33] there is little doubt that the position of the urban wage-earner deteriorated. Dr Jansen has documented the widespread extent of poverty in Amsterdam in the later eighteenth century,[34] and the close correlation which existed between the level of mortality, the number of marriages, and the price of bread during a period in which the trend of rye prices was moving steadily upwards.[35] His results demonstrate beyond doubt the 'preindustrial character' of economic crises in Holland at the end of the eighteenth century, and indicate that 'apart from increasing foreign competition, high grain prices must have played a significant role in the Republic's rapid economic decline during the last quarter of the eighteenth century.'[36]

There is much to suggest, therefore, that historians have exaggerated the extent to which the decline of the Baltic grain trade damaged the Dutch economy during the first half of the eighteenth century, given the readjustments which were taking place within the structure of Dutch-Baltic trade. Moreover, the revival of that trade offered little that was propitious to general economic recovery. More important than the *source* of grain imports was the *price* at which that grain could be imported. In this context, the period of bulk import of subsidised English grain particularly in what might be termed the 'second phase' of export from *c.* 1732 to 1760, should be seen as a positive one for the highly vulnerable Dutch economy.

Not only, of course, did this price-vulnerability encompass food imports, it also extended to imports of industrial raw materials and here, it is evident that the import of heavily subsidised English malt provided the basis for the rapid expansion of the Dutch distilleries during the early eighteenth century. We have already seen how the conjuncture of the English bounty legislation and excise regulations with the technical requirements of Dutch distillers produced an irresistably cheap raw material which gave rise to a period of exceptionally rapid growth in the distilleries of the Maas region.[37] At Schiedam, the centre of the industry, the number of distilleries increased from thirty-four in 1700 to 121 in 1730, reaching 122 by 1771.[38] As a result, Schiedam was one of the few industrial towns in Holland to experience any increase in population during the eighteenth century.[39] In Rotterdam, the *Vroedschap* passed a resolution in 1718 setting aside the Baan for the distillers, and the industry also flourished in Delfshaven. It is thus not surprising that by mid-century, grain-spirits formed one of the principal exports of the Maas region, finding markets in England, France and Spain, the East and West Indies, and North America: by the early 1770s, 85 per cent of total output was exported.[40] The remarkable growth of this export-oriented industry must therefore be seen as one of the most conspicuous exceptions to the Republic's industrial history in the eighteenth century, and it is perhaps significant that this was due to circumstances external to its own economic situation – the cheapness of imported raw materials – rather than to the unique quality of the product, as Joh. de Vries has suggested.[41]

The Dutch brewing industry also received a proportion of its malt and barley from England during the same period but was not nearly as dependent upon English supplies as the distilleries, since English Maltsters and merchants found it most profitable to export 'long malt' which could only be used in the latter. In any case, the brewing industry in Holland was one of the oldest of the processing industries and for most of the eighteenth century was in a state of decline in the face of contracting markets. The growth of foreign competition, increasing consumption of coffee, tea and spirits, and heavy internal taxation – there were no less than seven taxes on beer – were the main elements in the situation.[42]

While distillers and, to a small extent, brewers, obviously benefitted from imports of English grain, the Dutch malting industry was adversely affected by English competition. Dutch maltsters continually pressed for increased protection against English malt exports and in 1725, an already low duty of 3.15 guilders per last was increased to 5.0 gl. Even the Amsterdam Admiralty supported the maltsters in their attempt to secure a tariff reduction on imported barley, although this was not implemented until 1751.[43] Since the level of import duties was, by English standards extremely low, it is likely that these adjustments had only a marginal effect. But if, as has been argued, the expansion of the Dutch distilleries was itself a consequence of the growth of heavily subsidised East Anglian malt exports, it cannot be said that the Dutch malting industry suffered unduly. The growth of this trade, in other words, largely created its own demand, and it was the contracting requirements of the declining brewing industry which presented a more serious threat. When English malt exports were cut off during the years of harvest failure in 1757/8, the industry revived, as the English agent in Rotterdam explained:[44]

> The total prohibition of export from England in 1757 and 1758 demonstrated very plainly that the Dutch could do without the English malt; cut off by this measure from their usual supply, the Dutch were set upon building a number of malt houses all over the country, which they continue to keep at work with success. The price of their own barley enables them to make malt much cheaper than it can be imported from England; and the distillers and major part of the brewers are almost wholly supplied with their own inland malt.

On balance therefore, Dutch industry can only have benefitted from the import of subsidised malt and barley, and far from damaging the Dutch economy, the import of English cereals probably helped to sustain its specialised rural sector at a time when other influences were tending to depress Dutch agriculture.

VI Grain Exports and the English Economy

At the risk of stating the obvious, it must be pointed out that the place of grain exports in the structure of the English economy was entirely different from the more dominant position which the Dutch Republic's grain trade occupied in relation to its more specialised agriculture and to its economy as a whole. Although England's grain surplus was at times sizable during this period, it was none the less a marginal one, representing between one-thirtieth and one-twelfth of total domestic grain production. In estimating the impact of grain exports on the English economy, it will be convenient to consider the benefits which allegedly accrued to the English economy as a result of the trade, before indicating the economic and social costs involved. The trade's contribution to overseas earnings, the stimulus which it provided for the shipping industry, and the enhancement of prices in the interests of producers will form the main components of this rough balance sheet.

The fact that the price of grain was subject to both wide annual fluctuations and considerable variations in quality within any given period means that the contribution of the trade to the balance of payments can be estimated only with considerable difficulty. Although institutional price series for grain sold on the domestic market are readily available, especially for wheat, real prices for grain entering into the international trade are scarce; while the Inspector General's official values are of limited usefulness for this purpose, particularly if it is desired to arrive at an estimate for any specific year. William Culliford, the first Inspector General of Imports and Exports, must have been especially conscious of this kind of problem when making his annual revision of official values from 1696/7 until 1701, as the bad harvests and high prices of the

1690s gave way to the lower prices of the early 1700s. From 1701 Culliford and his successors abandoned the attempt to revise the list of official values and these became fossilised at the then existing levels for the remainder of the century, with very few exceptions.[1]

A comparison of the official values with actual prices of English grain sold in Holland, made in Table 7, indicates that the discrepancy is most serious in the case of malt, which, at 17s 6d per quarter, was substantially over-valued. Prices of wheat exports, however, approximated much more closely to the official valuation of 27s per quarter, although pronounced fluctuations could occur. Rye, oatmeal and barley prices were much more stable than wheat prices, and as these grains played only a minor role in the export trade, any discrepancy between the official values and real prices would not introduce a serious element of distortion. In arriving at an estimate of the annual average contribution of grain exports to overseas earnings therefore, it is proposed to make use of the official values for these three grains only. In the case of wheat, a decennial average price derived from London (Bear Quay) prices will be utilised in an attempt to take some account of price fluctuations, since the level of prices at this market seems to correspond fairly closely to those obtained for English wheat sold on the Amsterdam Bourse. (A complete series for the latter unfortunately does not exist). It has already been pointed out that freight and handling charges for English grain carried to nearby Europe were absorbed by the bounty, and it is this which accounts for the comparability in the level of prices between the two markets. In the case of malt, a more realistic figure of 10s will be substituted for the official valuation of 17s 6d in the light of the price data in Table 7 and the various contemporary comments on the scale of abuses in the malt trade, quoted earlier. In 1717, the Excise Office claimed that Norfolk exporters were 'enabled to sell their malt in Holland for half the price that they pay for their barley in England', that is, from five to ten shillings per quarter.[2] While this official view may underestimate the value of malt exports, especially after the legislative changes of the later 1720s, it is likely that the prices shown in Table 7, taken as they are from the published *prijscouranten*, relate to a better quality product than that supplied direct to the distillers.

Table 7: Prices of English and Baltic Grains
sold in Holland, 1714–63

Shillings and pence per quarter

Official values for grain exported from England and Wales, from 1701: Wheat 27/-, Rye 18/6, Oatmeal 12/-, Malt 17/6, Barley 17/-, stabilised at 13/- from 1703.

I Rotterdam[1]

	English Wheat	Polish Wheat	English Malt	(London BQ)[2]
1715 May	26/5	37/3	13/6	27/-
	English Rye	Prussian Rye		
	18/10	24/10		

II Amsterdam Bourse[1]

	English Wheat	Polish Wheat	English Malt	(London BQ/ML)[2]
1722 Nov.	—	—	7/1	—
1736 Apr.–May	—	—	10/1	—
1739 Jan.–Mar.	24/5	27/2	9/3	28/3
			(Dutch Malt, 12/6)	
1747 Oct.	28/-	32/7	14/1	26/9
1748 Jan.–Mar.	—	—	—	—
Apr.–June	29/4	33/8	12/2	29/-
July–Sept.	28/9	30/5	12/1	27/4
Oct.–Dec.	35/5	34/6	14/2	29/3
1750 Jan.–Mar.	—	—	—	—
Apr.–June	27/10	31/5	11/8	28/9
July–Sept.	28/8	31/-	12/6	28/6
Oct.–Dec.	27/4	29/-	—	27/5
1754 May	24/2	24/4	—	25/11
1760 Jan.–Mar.	—	—	—	—
Apr.–June	25/2	—	—	26/5
July–Sept.	28/10	27/5	—	27/10
Oct.–Dec.	30/3	30/9	—	27/8

1761 Jan.–Mar.	27/10	30/10	—	23/5
Apr.–June	—	—	—	—
July–Sept.	—	—	—	—
Oct.–Dec.	29/9	30/4	—	23/6
1762 Jan.–Mar.	27/6	29/11	—	24/-
Apr.–June	—	—	—	—
July–Sept.	—	—	—	—
Oct.–Dec.	31/2	32/2	—	31/1
1763 Jan.–Mar.	29/8	31/8	—	30/2
Apr.–June	28/5	31/5	—	27/2
July–Sept.	—	—	—	—
Oct.–Dec.	—	—	—	—

III Amsterdam, Exported from Hull by Henry Maister
English Wheat   (London BQ)[2]

1714 Nov.	29/10	32/-
Dec.	31/6	28/-
1715 Jan.	28/-	28/6
Mar.	27/6	28/6

Notes and Sources

[1] Prices converted into sterling at current (monthly) Amsterdam rate.

[2] London prices (Bear Quay until 1754. Mark Lane from 1760) are shown for comparison.

Quotations under I and II are taken from price-currents assembled for the Nederlandsch Instituut voor Prijsgeschiedenis by N. W. Posthumus, now deposited in the Economisch-Historisch Bibliotheek, Amsterdam. The series for Polish Wheat was published in Posthumus, *Nederlandsche Prijsgeschiedenis*, I (Leiden 1943) pp. 4–8. Where a range of quotations is given in the original, the mid-point is quoted above.

Quotations under III are taken from the Maister Ledger, deposited in Hull University Library, DP/82.

On this basis then, the annual average contribution of grain exports to England's visible trade balance may be estimated as follows, bearing in mind that no element has been included to take account of freight and commission charges since these were subsidised via bounty payments and hence should properly be excluded from the net contribution of grain exports to overseas earnings:

Table 8: Estimated Average Annual Contribution of English Grain Exports to balance of Visible Trade, 1700s–1750s

	As % of English Produce and Manufactures only	*As % of Total English Exports (including Re-exports)*
1701–10	5.46	3.69
1711–20	7.48	5.10
1721–30	6.89	4.35
1731–40	9.17	5.92
1741–50	10.49	6.94
1751–60	6.48	4.63

These admittedly rough calculations, which incorporate a downward revision of malt values, would suggest that grain exports made a more modest contribution to England's visible trade balance than that indicated by Professor John, who accepted the official values and tended to focus attention on the peak years of export. At the same time, Professor John excluded re-exports from the picture, which naturally tends to exaggerate the significance of grain exports in English foreign trade. Yet both branches of trade were carefully fostered by specific pieces of mercantilist legislation and can be seen as comparable products of the commercial policy of the period. Although the rate of growth of grain exports was greater than that of re-exports during the first half of the eighteenth century, the substantially greater value of the latter means that its slower rate of expansion is nevertheless more impressive than that of grain exports and its contribution to the balance of payments more substantial, in spite of the falling prices of plantation goods in the 1720s and 1730s.[3] Expressed as a percentage of total commodity exports it can be seen that grain provided only a marginal contribution to overseas earnings ranging from an annual average of 3.7 per cent in the early years of the century to 6.9 per cent in the peak decade of the 1740s (which includes the peak year of 1750).

These averages, of course, conceal considerable annual variations determined mainly by the size of the harvest. The large surpluses of 1734, 1738 and late 1740s and early 1750s were, however no less exceptional than the shortages and high prices of the years 1709/10, 1728, 1740 and 1757/8.[4]

As far as the trade's shipping requirements are concerned, it is clear that the bulk of English grain was carried to overseas markets in English ships, a situation deliberately encouraged by the provisions of the bounty legislation. But because freight and handling charges were heavily subsidised by bounty payments, and the benefit of the subsidy passed on to overseas consumers in the form of lower prices,[5] it seems that the net contribution of freight earnings must have been slight or non-existent. There may, however, have been benefits of a less direct kind. It is at least possible that increased investment in the shipping industry, necessitated by the growing volume of grain exports, may have produced important multiplier effects throughout the industry and the economy; and further, that the trade may have stimulated greater commercial activity by drawing in return cargoes.

How much shipping, in fact, was required for grain exports, and how did the demands of English exporters compare with those of Dutch exporters of Baltic grain? As Professor Davis has shown, the tonnage of shipping required for grain exports was exceeded only by that required for overseas coal shipments.[6] But those contemporaries, like Defoe, who argued that the corn trade employed more shipping 'than will be thought probable at first sight' tended to exaggerate,[7] and it is evident that the shipping requirements of English exporters were less substantial than those of Dutch-Baltic traders, in terms of an equivalent measure of grain, for two reasons.

In the first place, the majority of English grain voyages were a good deal shorter than those from the Baltic. On average, between two-thirds and three-quarters of all grain voyages consisted of short hauls from London and East Anglia to nearby Europe so that small vessels, usually between 80 and 90 tons, manned by small crews, were characteristic of the former.[8] Such vessels could complete several voyages during the course of a year. Grain was usually shipped in bulk and charter-parties rarely specified more than four or six working days for loading; Nathaniel Maister of Hull, for example, observed that 180 to 200 quarters of grain per day could be shipped in good weather.[9] The Dutch-Baltic trade, on the other hand, consisted of long and relatively expensive voyages, involving carriage from Danzig to Amsterdam, handling and warehousing charges in the latter, and transhipment to final markets. Baltic carriers were therefore substantially larger than English grain vessels, averaging just over 160 tons during the first half of the eighteenth century[10]

In the second place, English exports contained a high proportion of malt which required considerably less shipping space – perhaps as much as 40 per cent less – than the bread grains wheat and rye of which the Baltic grain trade almost entirely consisted. This was carefully explained by the Collector of Customs at Yarmouth in 1738.[11]

> A quarter of barley will fill up less room in a ship than a quarter of wheat & the reason we take to be from the form of each respective grain, barley laying lighter in a bushel than wheat; when it is poured into a ships hold, settles closer than it did in the bushel & the proportion is generally accounted as 11 to 10 & that rule has long been observed here ... . We are informed that a quarter of malt well made fine and fit for [the] London market will take up as much room in stowage as a quarter of barley, but malt for [the] Holland markets, which in making is suffered to run out to a very great length on the floors, after it is measured into a ship may be much easier compressed; besides malt being so much lighter than corn & stowed in bulk, the ships hold is generally filled quite up to the beams & for the Holland markets they force it closely into every part of the hold. For an instance hereof we humbly refer to the ship *Peach* . . . the ship is reported by the master at 60 tons, but we judge her at upwards of 90; in the coal trade she make[s] about 80 chalders coals Winchester measure & carries about 400 quarters of wheat; but with malt for Rotterdam she generally clears out with 700 quarters and upwards & we are well satisfied the whole is actually on board.

If this report is reliable (and the circumstances in which it was presented suggest that it is), then it is clear that the trade made more modest demands upon shipping than might otherwise be supposed, particularly in the first phase of export up to *c.* 1730 when East Anglian malt shipments predominated. By applying the above proportions to the Inspector General's statistics, the shipping tonnage employed in the bulk export trades may be estimated as follows:[12]

Table 9: Shipping Tonnage Employed in the English Overseas Coal and Grain Trades, 1700s–1750s
Annual Averages ('000 tons)

	Coal	Grain
1701–10	71	51
1711–20	113	66
1721–30	157	68
1731–40	185	100
1741–50	200	152
1751–60	221	105

Because overseas coal shipments were subject to heavy duties, under-declaration of exports was widespread, so that the above figures doubtless underestimate the real volume of shipping tonnage in the coal trade especially in relation to that for grain exports which, if anything, would be subject to over-declaration in view of the temptation to obtain excess bounty payments. There is therefore no doubt that the shipping requirements of the grain trade were much less substantial than those of the overseas coal trade, while the combined needs of both were overshadowed by the vast tonnage employed in the domestic coal trade from the north-eastern ports to London, which averaged between 450 and 550 thousand tons per year during the first half of the eighteenth century.[13]

In specific years however, particularly the later 1740s and early 1750s, the quantity of shipping required for grain exports could be considerable. 'Some years past', wrote the British agent in Rotterdam, in 1765, 'we have had from 800 to one thousand of these vessels (i.e.

entries) here in a year', and 'from 50 to 60 corn ships have been known here at a time.'[14] During peak years such as these, corn vessels would be supplemented by shipping drawn from the coal and Norway trades, since the seasonal pattern of these trades dovetailed.[15] Activity in the coal trade remained at a low level throughout the winter months. Ralph Carr explained that he never shipped coal 'unless the weather is dry and the coals newly wrought, which very seldom happens but in summer time, for as these coals is never laid under any cover, they become as heavy as lead by the rains so would less [lose] 3/- p. [per] chaldron by their weighing so much.'[16]

The trade in bread grains, in contrast, was brisk from September until March.[17] By early Spring, the countries of southern Europe were gathering in the harvest so that demand from that quarter, which in turn affected the demands of Dutch merchants for English grain, was slack throughout the summer months. A number of merchants therefore engaged in both these branches of bulk export, such as William Cotesworth of Newcastle, William Konink of Rotterdam, and Carr himself.[18]

The seasonality of trade patterns is an aspect of economic history which has sometimes been neglected, but in this instance, it explains how a part of the shipping requirements of a virtually new bulk cargo were satisfied. The major stimulus behind the expansion of shipping tonnage in England's trade with Europe in this period was undoubtedly that provided by the long-established coal export trade, but the appearance of a fluctuating though expanding grain surplus meant that this increasing tonnage could be used more intensively.[19] Charter-parties in the Rotterdam notarial archives contain several examples of vessels which operated in both the coal and grain trades during the course of the year, such as the 70-ton *Nancy* of Shields which in November 1734 was chartered to 'load unspecified goods at Rotterdam, thence to Bridlington Key to lie 48 hours to receive orders whether to complete [her] load with corn from thence or to proceed to Sunderland or Newcastle to load coal; thence to Christiansand to unload and reload with unspecified goods, thence back to Rotterdam to unload.'[20] During years of grain shortage in England, it was common for Sunderland vessels exporting coal to Rotterdam to return with grain cargoes to the western ports or London;[21] and conversely it is possible to find examples of Yarmouth and Blakeney vessels, which normally carried grain cargoes, operating in the coal trade.[22]

While the shipping requirements of these two branches of trade were to some extent complementary, the fact remains that their simultaneous expansion did lead to an overall scarcity of outward shipping space, especially during wartime. In an admittedly difficult year, 1738, Ralph Carr was 'obliged to write to all the ports round us to procure small vessels for the corn trade at any rate',[23] and ten years later, John Coutts of Edinburgh was complaining that there was 'no shipping here for carrying out our corns.'[24] The Maisters experienced similar problems and insisted that masters signed a note binding them whilst the charter-party was being drawn up.[25]

During wartime, English freights could rise prodigiously and English exporters took advantage of the lower rates and greater security offered by neutral shipping, particularly that of Holland, Denmark and Sweden during the conflicts of 1740 and the period 1756 to 1763.[26] In April 1740, Carr was certain that Dutch shipping was available at a 'much lower fraught than ours' and subsequently informed his agent at Dunkirk that he was expecting 'sundry more foreign ships' to load for the Bay of Biscay, and five others coming to load for Holland. The lower freight charges, he calculated 'within a trifle' balanced against the loss of bounty and higher duty consequent upon shipment of grain and coal in foreign vessels.[27] In some cases, it is probable that the identity of foreign vessels was concealed in order to secure payment of bounties, since the Inspector General's office returned suspiciously low figures for foreign vessels employed in the grain trade which, in the light of merchants' correspondence and the remarks of pamphleteers would seem to be misleading.[28] In 1765, the British agent in Rotterdam, Richard Wolters, complained that 'In time of war, the number of Dutch ships to the British ports was very considerable owing to the high price of assurance upon British bottoms, and dilatoriness of convoy', and went on to suggest, as certain pamphleteers did, that the export of bounty and debenture goods should be limited to British vessels. The grain trade was singled out as one which would benefit especially from such a limitation.[29]

A further consideration which encouraged the use of neutral shipping during wartime was the problem of trading with the enemy. In 1747, when there was said to be a 'great want' of wheat in France, exacerbated by the depredations of English privateers in the Mediterranean which had cut off French imports from the Levant, it was English grain supplies transported in Dutch and Danish ships which, paradoxically, made good the deficiency. Richard Wolters believed that most of this grain was exported on the accounts of Rotterdam merchants and reported that 'Dutch ships are daily freighted to go to England to take in a cargo part in lead and the rest in wheat or coals, which are all very welcome in France.'[30]

A number of factors operated, therefore, to increase the proportion of foreign shipping employed in the grain trade during wartime and hence to reduce freight earnings – especially during the peak years of export in the later 1740s. Furthermore, it must be emphasised that the enormous volume of outward grain shipments was not, throughout the entire period, matched by anything like a comparable volume of imports. Masters and owners of corn vessels experienced great difficulty in securing return cargoes, and the problem of imbalance was heightened by the even larger outward shipments of coal to the same markets in nearby and southern Europe.[31] There were, however, two alternatives to returning in ballast: the legal one of engaging in a triangular trade of some sort and the illegal one of smuggling, and it seems that both were resorted to by corn and coal traders. In 1715, the Collector of Customs at Yarmouth noted that 'our corn vessels bound for Holland mostly return light home and . . . bring small parcels of goods which they run to the northwards of us.'[32] The smuggling trade with France and Holland was indeed brisk during the first half of the eighteenth century, but masters in the corn and coal trades were involved only peripherally. Smuggling was in general a highly organised activity undertaken by wholesale merchants, engaging in virtually no other activity and operating specially built well-armed cutters.[33] Triangular trade was probably a more satisfactory solution to the problem. A pamphlet of 1750 claimed that 'many of our corn ships, whose cargoes being landed in the Mediterranean, or other places . . . proceed thence to British America in ballast, in order to procure a lading home.'[34] Merchants disposing of grain in Norwegian and Swedish ports normally had no difficulty in securing return cargoes of timber and iron, but such voyages formed a relatively small component of the total grain export trade.[35] In fact the Rotterdam charter-parties suggest that the overwhelming majority of English and Dutch corn vessels left Rotterdam either in ballast or with a light loading on the master's account. In this sense, the grain trade was highly unbalanced and the shortage of return cargoes made for relatively high outward freight rates. It seems that the trade did not, as one grain exporter had hoped, 'bring so many other things along with it' in either direction.[36]

If the trade made only a limited contribution to the balance of payments and provided a less profound stimulus to the shipping industry than some contemporaries claimed, it must be remembered that the rationale underlying the policy of subsidised grain export was, in the first instance, shaped by agrarian rather than commercial interests. As we have already noticed, that policy represented 'a convention between the government and the landed interest, to which the commercial body, though materially affected by it, were not parties'[37] since its purpose was to help landowners shoulder the burden of the land tax.[38] Of course contemporary landowners and their spokesmen, such as Arthur Young, denied that the effect of the bounty was to raise prices.[39] The content of this polemical literature, which grew in response to attacks against the Corn Laws mounted from *c.* 1750, has been indicated by D. G. Barnes, and the fallacies upon which it rested have been effectively laid bare, as we have seen, by C. R. Fay and T. S. Ashton. It is unnecessary to recapitulate their arguments here, but Fay's conclusion is worth quoting: the bounty, he wrote 'raised home prices and raised landlords' rents a little, cost the Treasury more than it could afford, kept the farmer in good heart, and provided succeeding generations with abundant food for erroneous reasoning in speech, tract, and treatise.'[40] To the extent that grain exports benefitted landowners and farmers by raising rents and prices, they must have damaged those industrial producers who relied upon grain products for their raw materials; and in raising the price of basic foodstuffs, they must have tended towards higher wage costs. These considerations, of course, lay at the heart of the struggle over the repeal of the nineteenth-century Corn Laws, but in the third quarter of the eighteenth century they were voiced by only a small 'industrial interest' composed mainly of brewers and distillers. It was Michael Combrune, a brewer, who provided perhaps the most effective and informed challenge to the arguments advanced by the landed interest in favour of the bounty, in his *Enquiry* of 1768.[41] Although his political arithmetic can only be described as eccentric, it did at least provide a more realistic conspectus of the likely effects of the bounty than the calculations of Sir Charles Smith which simply deducted the costs of the bounty and occasional grain imports from the total value of grain exports to produce a substantial net gain;[42] or of Arthur Young who asserted that the value of grain exports for the period 1745 to 1750 was 'equivalent in national advantage to 22 million pounds raised by manufactures exported when the materials are not of our own production'.[43] As well as the costs of the bounty, grain imports, and the drawback of malt duties, Combrune also took into account price increases for provisions other than grain, resulting from a 'diminution of pasture', as well as higher grain prices themselves; and he was aware of abuses in the malt trade, and pointed to the possibility of increased wage costs resulting from higher food prices.[44]

Although it is impossible to estimate the exact extent of these influences, something more can be said about the alleged effects of the bounty in moderating the scale of fluctuations in grain prices and in relieving scarcity. Its supporters argued that it encouraged 'the farmer to keep a larger stock by him in a cheap time, for a vent either abroad or at home'; and because it raised the price of grain in years of plenty, 'the farmer can afford to sell the cheaper when the harvests fail: for their mean or medium price must be secured.'[45] But, as we have already noticed, the bounty operated at a fixed rate in good and bad seasons alike and therefore tended to drive the entire surplus overseas during good years. This merely heightened

the shortages of poor harvest years, by which time temporary sus-
pension of the bounty and prohibition of export could provide
only a limited stabilising influence. By specifying the price levels at
which grain could be exported and imported the legislation
appeared to lay down minimal controls to safeguard the interests of
consumers; but the relatively high levels which were fixed in the late
seventeenth century rendered these controls virtually inoperative
in conditions of lower prices which characterised the first half of the
eighteenth. In any case, there was no machinery for determining
the prices of grain at ports of export, and that for controlling import
was ineffective.[46] Professor Barnes concluded that the *ad hoc* and
unauthorised methods which were actually adopted by customs
officers were unsatisfactory and open to frauds.[47]

International comparison of eighteenth-century wheat prices
indicates that fluctuations in the London market were no less pronounced than those in various other European centres where no
bounty system was in operation, such as Amsterdam, Leipzig, and
Ancona – although these markets were a good deal more stable
than those of northern France and northern Spain which were still
subject to periodic subsistence crises (figure 5).[48] It must be remembered too that London was the most amply supplied grain market
in England, and was therefore less subject to wide fluctuations in
prices than inland markets with poor communications. Although it
has been suggested that the autonomy of wheat markets has been
overstated for the first half of the eighteenth century,[49] there is no
doubt that the surpluses of the south-east entered the overseas
grain market in preference to the domestic market, and so did little
to relieve the recurrent shortages of the western counties. As
Combrune remarked, 'the navigation from Norfolk to Holland is
much shorter than to the western parts of England, where then
[1757–8] a real scarcity existed.' The most effective way for farmers
to keep up prices, he continued 'was not to supply the other parts of
England, but to send it abroad.'[50] The returns made to the Commissioners for Trade and Plantations during one of the most acute
years of shortage, 1709, show that London and south-eastern wheat
prices were moderate compared with those prevailing in the south-

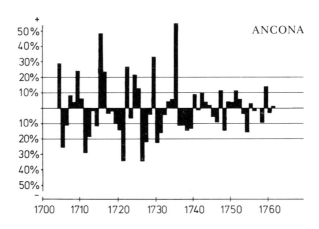

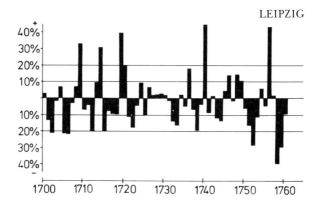

Figure 5: Fluctuations in European Wheat Prices, 1700–60
(Annual percentage deviation from nine year moving average)
Sources: See chapter VI, note 48

west (figure 6).[51] The lower level of wheat prices observed in the north-east and north-west is probably explained by a shift towards rye consumption as wheat prices rose.[52]

The evidence of price fluctuations indicates therefore that the bounty legislation did little to ensure that the home market was well

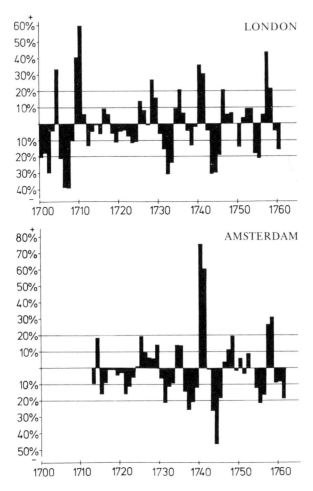

Figure 5 (cont.)

supplied with grain at all times, indeed, it may have tended to withdraw grain from domestic consumption. Had the subsidy been applied instead to the building of public granaries and internal transport improvements, as some critics suggested it might have been, a more satisfactory level of prices would doubtless have been

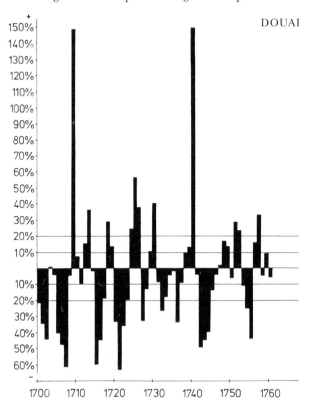

Figure 5: Fluctuations in European Wheat Prices, 1700–60
(Annual percentage deviation from nine year moving average)
Sources: See chapter VI, note 48

achieved, while easing some of the problems faced by producers during periods of low prices. In response to this kind of criticism, supporters of the bounty argued that larger farmers themselves 'in some measure serve at their own private expense the same purpose as public magazines'[53] although the substantial reliance placed on grain imports during years of scarcity suggests otherwise. There is also much literary evidence, some of which was quoted by D. G. Barnes, which indicates that 'The old fear of starvation, with its cen-

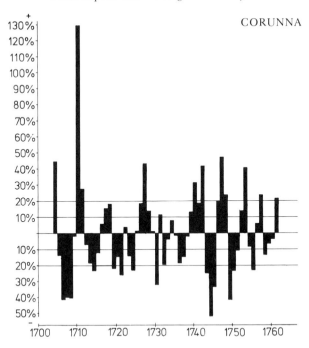

Figure 5 (cont.)

turies of tradition, was aroused in many parts of the country by this very exportation.'[54] Even during the plentiful years of the 1730s, many instances were cited in the *Gentleman's Magazine* in which mobs plundered corn dealers or attempted to prevent export, and, in 1737, an act was passed laying down heavy penalties including hard labour, public whipping and transportation against those using violence to hinder the purchase or carriage of grain.[55] In 1740 when grain shortages reached crisis proportions and rioting was widespread, magistrates were ordered to enforce the 1552 act against forestalling, engrossing and regrating – an interesting indication that Parliament preferred to apply an already existing law (designed in quite different circumstances) rather than to tamper with the more recent legislation encouraging export.[56]

No full-length account of eighteenth-century grain riots is yet

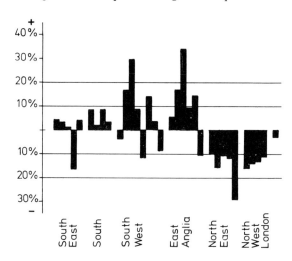

Figure 6: Fluctuations in Wheat Prices at English Ports, 1709
(Percentage deviation from average price)
Sources: See chapter VI, note 51

available so that the true extent of such disturbances is not known, but preliminary investigations indicate a total of 56 recorded food protests during the period 1660 to 1737, 84 during 1740 alone, over 140 in thirty different counties during the crisis of 1756 and 1757, and over 170 during 1766.[57] Leaving aside the problem of unrecorded incidents, the total of known disturbances provides only a partial reflection of the distress and hardship experienced during years of shortage because local magistrates tended to rely on informers when rioting seemed imminent and hence were able to take preventative measures. In May 1728 for example, following the Cornish tinners' riots, John Pye, mayor of Falmouth and himself a grain exporter, obtained information indicating the threat of a second attack and promptly demanded two detachments of troops and the presence of a man-of-war in Falmouth harbour. Their arrival succeeded in averting further rioting, if only temporarily. Early in 1729, the tinners again roamed the Cornish countryside searching for corn. The magistrates and gentry of Cornwall

petitioned the Secretaries of State for the issue of a royal procla-
mation for 'the capture of notorious rioters', and with the arrival of
a stronger military force, the rioting ceased. A similar sequence of
events recurred in 1737, a year of substantial export. 'I am told',
wrote one of Pye's informers, 'you have bought up a large quantity
of corn lately, which has been the means of raising the price of corn
to such a degree, as to incense the tinners so much against you and
your family that I am credibly informed no less than a thousand of
them will be with you tomorrow early: they are first to assemble at
Chacewater and then to proceed for Falmouth. This I am told was
publicly declared at Redruth market last Friday (not but that I've
heard it reported before that the tinners were going to pay you a
visit).' A forty-gun ship and a body of troops were again called for
and Pye himself organised a guard of the Falmouth townspeople
and informed Rolfey and Wood, the London merchants with
whom he was doing business, that they would have to bear the
expense of this guard in an increase in the price of corn supplied to
them.[58] As a group of industrial workers who were dependent upon
the market for food purchases, the Cornish tinners continued to
play a prominent part in eighteenth-century grain riots. In 1793,
large numbers of them collected at Falmouth to demand fixed
grain prices, before marching round the county to enforce a general
reduction of prices.[59]

Although eighteenth-century food riots took various forms,[60] the
Cornish riots illustrate certain common characteristics of these disturbances over the country as a whole. In the first place, they were
in most instances easily suppressed by military forces; the widespread and prolonged disturbances of 1740 were in this respect
exceptional. Secondly, merchants supplying the export trade were
commonly singled out for attack since it was believed, rightly or
wrongly, that grain export was often responsible for high prices;
and thirdly, local magistrates, who were the effective controlling
authority, were frequently themselves interested in grain export.
While exporting and hoarding probably raised prices in many
areas, it was, as in most pre-industrial societies, a combination of
bad harvests, natural scarcity, and imperfections in the internal
grain market which were primarily responsible for high food

prices. But in directing their actions against exporters, and in attempting to impose fixed prices on the market, it may be suggested that rioters were struggling against a new set of political conditions affecting food supply which were first experienced during the 1690s and which involved, 'on the one hand, a local magistracy no longer prepared to impose controls on the market and the dealers as in Tudor and early Stuart days, and on the other, a system of regulation designed explicitly to encourage exports, discourage imports and keep prices high.'[61]

Like the evidence provided by price fluctuations, that relating to grain riots suggests that the bounty legislation tended to exacerbate rather than alleviate problems of food supply during the period under consideration. At the same time, high mortality and checks to population growth, especially during the second quarter of the eighteenth century, may suggest some inadequacy in food supply. Ashton described the years 1708 to 1710, 1725 to 1729, and 1739 to 1742 as periods which saw sharp increases in the number of burials brought about by severe climatic conditions combined with hunger or ailments resulting from shortage of food.[62] In 1729, Dr Hillary of Ripon observed that in northern England, 'many of the little country towns and villages were almost stripped of their poor people . . . very few of the richer people, who used a more generous way of living and were not exposed to the inclemencies of the weather, were seized with any of these diseases at this time.'[63] William Stout of Lancaster noted in his autobiography that 1728 had been a hard year for the poor because of the deficient harvest and high corn prices, a 'very sickly summer and great mortality in the plain country, much more than in the towns; and the burials were double this year.'[64]

Some modern writers, such as Chambers, have argued that food shortages exercised little influence over the spread of disease and the level of mortality, and argue in favour of an 'autonomous death rate' moving quite independently of environmental changes.[65] The investigations of A. B. Appleby into grain prices and subsistence crises in France and England during the late seventeen and early eighteenth centuries suggested that the persistence of famine in France and its relative absence in England might be explained by the availability of cheaper grains in times of crisis: 'The secret in avoiding famine, it seems, was in a balanced agriculture, with wheat and/or rye constituting an important bread grain but with adequate oats and barley to fall back on in times of scarcity, as Malthus long ago pointed out.'[66] But Appleby's evidence sheds no light on the nature of the relationship between food supplies, ill health and resistance to disease, and draws mainly on price materials from Southern and Eastern England, mainly Winchester, Reading and Norwich. Appleby himself suggested that high oat and barley prices may have pushed up the number of burials in 1727/8 and that parts of the Midlands may have experienced subsistence crises during these years,[67] a view which agrees with those of contemporaries quoted above. Evidence collected by the Cambridge Group clearly shows that those broad fluctuations in the death rate characteristic of sixteenth-century England persisted until the 1750s, when a new stable pattern was permanently established.[68] Indeed, the most severe mortality crises of the entire early modern period occurred during the quarter century 1725/6 to 1749/50, marked, in the Cambridge Group's language, by four 'three-star' crises, in which surges in mortality were accompanied by falls in nuptiality and fertility.[69] The persistence of regional food shortages may or may not have contributed to the demographic recession of the 1720s and 1730s – the connection, if any, between these two phenomena has not yet been fully explored. But the historian cannot fail to notice that years which saw substantial exports of grain were followed by periods of scarcity, high prices, and rising levels of mortality, most notably during the crisis of the late 1720s, but also in 1740/1 which was more serious among the urban population.[70] The bounty legislation seems to have been particularly ineffective in dealing with the hardships of these crisis periods.

T. S. Ashton described the Corn Laws as a complicated body of legislation, 'the result of self-interest and prejudice'; and, 'like rulers in all ages', he wrote, 'the landlords who sat at Westminster tended to identify the interests of the nation with that of the class to which they belonged.'[71] The evidence indeed suggests that any benefits which derived from the late seventeenth-century Corn Laws and the grain export trade to which they gave rise accrued less to the economy as a whole than to certain sectional interests within it – to the landowning class in particular, and to those farmers who were more readily enabled to maintain their rent payments during a period of relatively depressed prices. It is doubtful whether the trade provided a strong spur to agrarian improvement, and while there was some stimulus to the shipping industry and a real contribution to the balance of payments, it seems that these were greatly overestimated by contemporaries. Agricultural writers and landowners tended, mainly for propagandist purposes, to exaggerate the stimulus which grain exports gave to agrarian improvement. In the pages of the *Gentleman's Magazine* and elsewhere, the bounty and the export trade were repeatedly justified in terms of improved farming and the lower level of prices which, it was argued, resulted: ''Tis by the bounty alone that our lands are improved, and so valuable a trade is gained to the kingdom, by which we are become, as it were, the chief granary of Europe, and by which so many millions of money have been brought into the nation, and the value of our lands so much increased.'[72] But rather than serving as a measure of the pace of agricultural innovation, the level of grain exports should be regarded as an indicator of the extent of landlords' and farmers' difficulties during a period of depression. As a device for raising prices, the policy of subsidised export undoubtedly had a positive, if somewhat limited effect; even during the 1740s however, when over eight million quarters of grain were shipped overseas, these massive exports failed to prevent prices from remaining low. By 1765, a disinterested observer could suggest that the bounty was:[73]

> merely a tax on the poor and prevents the natural price that the fair consumption would direct, and it seems far from the Landed Interest to give it encouragement because although it may nominally enhance the market price, yet the rate of the landlord's home consumption, the rate of labour, or (what is worse) the increase of the Poor Rates (attended too with a charge of a poor man's principles to despair and desperateness) more than over balance the augmented price occasioned by exportation. And if foreign markets will not from the honest natural turn of the times allow a proper gain to exporter and dealer, they ought not to

be served at the expense of the more happy and fertile country by making the poor there participate of foreign distress.

The importance of this episode in English commercial history should be viewed not only in real economic terms, though these were significant, but also as an indicator of those pressures and tendencies present in the early eighteenth-century English economy, of which the Corn Laws and subsidised grain export were an expression. In the first place, the evidence confirms much of what has already been written on the widespread and serious nature of agricultural depression during the first half of the eighteenth century, and especially from 1730 to 1750;[74] and it challenges the picture of a buoyant and responsive economy which Professor John sketched out for the same period, in opposition to arguments put forward by Chambers, Mingay, Habakkuk, Deane and Cole, Little, and others.[75] The condition of English farming and of the economy in general is best understood against the background of stagnation or contraction within the European economy during the century after 1650, and E. L. Jones is correct in suggesting that 'English agriculture responded to a basically similar, if less intense, phase of low cereal prices between approximately 1650 and 1750 with more success than continental countries.'[76] To the extent that English conditions were merely *less unfavourable* than elsewhere, a policy of subsidised grain export must be regarded as playing an important role in this process by bolstering up prices and therefore rents, and enabling farmers to stay in business. Wallerstein has argued that this represented a policy which involved the export of unemployment to other parts of Europe[77] or, as one contemporary opponent of the Corn Laws put it, 'To give a bounty on corn exported is . . . nothing less than to hire our people to work for foreigners.'[78] It was paralleled in the industrial and commercial sphere by a vigorous policy of import substitution from the 1690s onwards, when import duties on foreign linens, silks, paper and other products were raised to new higher levels. However the fact that England managed to improve its economic position in relative terms, by exporting its unemployment, hardly detracts from the overall situation of depression and stagnation.

In the second place, a policy of subsidised grain export can be seen as representing an essential element in the structure of agrarian capitalism designed to sustain that structure in a period of depression, during which the natural tendency of farm prices was downward. By subsidising the export of grain and discouraging imports, the English landowning class was attempting to raise grain prices and shift the terms of trade between agricultural and industrial products in favour of the former. But this amounted to more than the introduction of a new set of economic controls. It represented a determined political intervention by which basic foodstuffs were withdrawn from the sphere of the moral economy and placed firmly within a system of commodity production and exchange. The interests of both consumers and manufacturers were subordinated to those of farmers and landlords, although arguments linking the Corn Laws with agrarian improvement were devised by the latter to disguise the sectional basis of this policy.

In searching for the origins and essential characteristics of agrarian capitalism, historians have perhaps been too ready to define the phenomenon in terms of large-scale operations and the range of farming techniques practised, particularly certain 'key technological innovations',[79] against a background of buoyant investment. But capitalist agriculture can equally well develop in conditions of stagnation and depression, and efficiency is not its hallmark. The distinguishing characteristics of any mode of production must lie substantially in the conditions under which basic foodstuffs are produced and subsequently appropriated and distributed. In concentrating attention on the former – on methods of production and changing rural property relationships – recent commentators, following a tradition established by the Physiocrats, have made much of the contrast between the alleged backwardness of French peasant agriculture and the progressive, improving character of English farming based on the landlord-tenant relationship.[80] If, however, it is equally important to consider the mechanisms by which foodstuffs are appropriated and distributed, not only internally but internationally, then significant comparisons might be drawn between England and Holland. In both countries, the 'mercantile development of agriculture' was substantial and, as was suggested in chapter V, this involved some complementarity of interest between the two economies. But whereas the Dutch chose to develop a compact and specialised agricultural sector together with a high degree of international interdependence, involving massive grain imports,[81] the English chose agricultural self-sufficiency, protectionism, the abandonment of customary and social controls over food supply, and the manipulation of prices in the interests of producers by means of subsidised export.

The major difference between the two systems lay in the contrasting rôles played by merchant's capital. In the English case, the rôle of merchant's capital was to support and maintain the agricultural sector in its dominant position within the overall economic structure. In the Dutch case, it played a more independent rôle and approximated more closely to Marx's suggestion that merchant's capital is 'merely the intervening movement between extremes which it does not control and between premises which it does not create.'[82] The vulnerability of the eighteenth-century Dutch commercial economy and the resilience of agrarian capitalism in England during the same period is perhaps best understood in this light.

Appendix 1

Grain Exports from England and Wales, 1698–1760
Annual Figures, '000 quarters

	Malt & Barley	Wheat, Rye & Oatmeal		Malt & Barley	Wheat, Rye & Oatmeal
1698	2.1	8.3	*1722*	404.3	109.3
99	1.6	1.3	*23*	350.9	171.0
1700	63.5	76.7	*24*	252.2	269.8
01	72.4	142.5	*25*	307.8	226.4
02	88.1	142.0	*26*	355.9	162.4
03	194.8	165.2	*27*	250.1	41.7
04	133.6	119.8	*28*	195.5	5.2
05	158.8	120.3	*29*	135.4	23.0
06	151.3	238.3	*1730*	194.4	110.8
07	115.9	108.3	*31*	191.3	152.9
08	127.7	88.2	*32*	174.9	218.9
09	180.4	336.2	*33*	240.7	456.8
1710	85.3	26.3	*34*	303.3	512.0
11	148.4	115.2	*35*	277.3	156.6
12	211.5	163.2	*36*	199.5	120.6
13	270.5	216.2	*37*	127.4	471.4
14	238.9	195.4	*38*	259.3	618.5
15	108.4	197.9	*39*	246.3	310.4
16	241.5	115.8	*1740*	169.6	65.9
17	269.5	46.4	*41*	129.9	54.1
18	374.3	122.1	*42*	201.0	357.9
19	367.1	173.5	*43*	254.2	461.6
1720	258.0	135.8	*44*	239.9	307.8
21	350.6	151.9	*45*	315.2	418.6

	Malt & Barley	Wheat, Rye & Oatmeal		Malt & Barley	Wheat, Rye & Oatmeal
1746	440.7	196.6	*1754*	369.8	401.5
47	464.4	361.7	*55*	374.4	282.0
48	423.2	651.0	*56*	263.9	134.2
49	408.1	737.9	*57*	63.3	16.6
1750	555.3	1050.9	*58*	11.4	11.1
51	289.2	734.9	*59*	188.9	271.0
52	393.9	488.7	*1760*	258.8	445.9
53	341.5	331.5			

Source: Sir Charles Smith, *Three Tracts on the Corn Laws* (1766) pp. 107–12.

Appendix 2

London Wheat Prices, 1695–1760
Shillings and pence per quarter

1695	41/ 2	*1723*	27/–
96	55/ 2	*24*	28/10
97	46/ 8	*25*	37/ 8
98	53/ 2	*26*	35/ 9
99	19/ 9	*27*	32/ 8
1700	31/ 1	*28*	42/ 5
01	29/ 4	*29*	36/ 6
02	22/11	*1730*	28/ 4
03	28/–	*31*	25/ 6
04	36/ 2	*32*	20/ 9
05	23/ 4	*33*	21/10
06	20/ 2	*34*	30/ 2
07	21/ 6	*35*	33/ 5
08	32/ 3	*36*	31/ 5
09	51/–	*37*	29/ 7
1710	60/ 8	*38*	27/ 8
11	42/–	*39*	29/11
12	36/–	*1740*	39/ 5
13	39/ 8	*41*	36/ 3
14	39/ 2	*42*	26/ 5
15	33/ 5	*43*	19/ 4
16	37/ 4	*44*	19/ 4
17	35/ 6	*45*	21/ 5
18	30/ 2	*46*	30/ 4
19	27/ 2	*47*	27/ 1
1720	28/10	*48*	28/ 9
21	29/ 2	*49*	28/ 9
22	28/–	*1750*	25/ 3

1751	29/11
52	32/ 6
53	34/ 9
54	26/11
55	26/ 4
56	35/ 2
57	46/ 8
58	38/11
59	31/–
1760	28/ 5

Source: M. Combrune, *An Enquiry into the Prices of Wheat, Malt, and Occasionally of Other Provisions* (1768)

Appendix 3 (i)

The First Corn Bounty Act, 1672
(*Statutes of the Realm,* V, pp. 752, 781–2, 25 Ch. II, c. 1)

An Act for Raising the Sum of £1,238,750 for Supply of His Majesty's Extraordinary Occasions

Reasons for passing this Act.

W E your Majesty's most dutiful and loyal subjects the Commons assembled in Parliament, acknowledging with all humility and thankfulness your Majesty's abundant care for our preservation, and being deeply sensible of that extraordinary charge and expense with which your Majesty's present occasions are to be supported, have cheerfully and unanimously given and granted, and do hereby give and grant unto your most excellent Majesty, the sum of twelve hundred thirty eight thousand seven hundred and fifty pounds, to be raised and levied in manner following. And do humbly beseech your Majesty that it may be enacted and be it enacted by the King's most excellent Majesty, by and with the advice and consent of the Lords Spiritual and Temporal and of the Commons in this present Parliament assembled and by the authority of the same, that the sum of twelve hundred thirty eight thousand seven hundred and fifty pounds shall be raised, levied, and paid unto your Majesty within the space of eighteen months in manner following, that is to say, the sum of threescore and eight thousand eight hundred and nineteen pounds and nine shillings by the month for eighteen months beginning from the fourth day of February one thousand six hundred seventy and two shall be assessed, taxed, collected, levied, and paid by six quarterly payments in the several counties, cities, boroughs, towns, and places within England and Wales, and the town of Berwick upon Tweed, according to the several rates and proportions and in such manner as is hereafter expressed, that is to say, for every month of the said eighteen months.

Grant of £1,238,750.

To be raised within 18 months, at the times, in manner, and on the counties, etc. herein mentioned.

For the County of Bedford the sum of eight hundred ninety six pounds seventeen shillings and nine pence.

For the County of Berks. the sum of one thousand one hundred thirty two pounds six shillings and seven pence.

For the County of Bucks. the sum of one thousand three hundred and fifteen pounds six shillings and five pence. [etc.] . . .

And to the end that all owners of land whereupon this tax principally lieth may be the better enabled to pay the same by rendering the labours of the husbandman in raising corn and grain more valuable by exportation of the same into foreign parts which now is already at a very low rate, and that the nation in general may have her stock increased by the returns thereof, be it further enacted that for the space of three years from the first day of this session of Parliament and from thenceforward to the end of the next session of Parliament, when malt or barley (Winchester measure) is or shall be at twenty four shillings a quarter, rye thirty two shillings a quarter, and wheat forty eight shillings a quarter or under in any port or ports of this kingdom

XXXI.
For three years, etc. when corn herein mentioned persons shipping for exportation to bring a certificate of quantity and quality of corn on oath to the commissioners, etc.

100

or dominion of Wales every merchant or other person who shall put on shipboard in English shipping (the master and two thirds of the mariners at least being his Majesty's subjects) any sorts of the corn aforesaid from any such ports where the rates shall not then be higher than as aforesaid with intent to export the said corn to parts beyond the seas, every such merchant or other person shall bring a certificate in writing under his or their hands containing the quantity and quality of corn so shipped to the farmers, commissioners, collectors, or other persons appointed or to be appointed by his Majesty, his heirs, or successors to collect the duties and rates arising by customs within any such port and upon proof made of any such certificate by one or more credible persons upon their oaths, which oaths the said commissioners or other persons are hereby authorized and required to administer, and upon bond given by every such merchant or other person in the sum of two hundred pounds at the least for every hundred tons of corn so shipped and so proportionably, that the said corn (danger of the seas excepted) shall be exported into parts beyond the seas and not be again landed in the kingdom of England, dominion of Wales, the islands of Guernsey or Jersey, or town of Berwick upon Tweed, every such merchant so shipping off any of the aforesaid corn and giving certificate and bond as aforesaid shall have and receive from such farmers, commissioners, collectors, or other persons in any port respectively where the same corn shall be so shipped, for every quarter of barley or malt, ground or unground, two shillings and six pence, for every quarter of rye, ground or unground, three shillings and six pence, for every quarter of wheat, ground or unground, five shillings, which sum or sums every such commissioner, farmer, or other persons are hereby authorized and required upon demand by such exporter to make present payment of accordingly, without taking or requiring any thing for custom or any fee or reward for corn so laden to be exported, or for so much grain as shall be exported in any ship wherein any other goods shall be shipped; any law, statute, or usage in any wise to the contrary notwithstanding. And upon certificate returned under the common seal of the chief magistrate in any place or places beyond the seas, or under the hands and seals of two known English merchants upon the place that such corn was there landed, or upon proof by credible persons that such corn was taken by enemies or perished in the seas, the examination and proof thereof being left to the judgement of such commissioners, farmers, or other persons; which proof being made or certificate delivered to such person or persons respectively as took bond as aforesaid, the said bond shall be delivered up to such importer or his order to be cancelled without any fee for the same; and the moneys by any such commissioners, farmers, collector, or other person so paid in obedience to this act shall be accepted of in his or their accompts as so much paid to his Majesty, and he and they is and shall be discharged thereof accordingly . . .

Marginalia:

And thereupon, and upon bond given not to Ireland the same corn, etc.

To receive the bounties herein mentioned without fee;

and upon certificate of corn being duly landed, bond to be delivered up to exporter to be cancelled without fee;

and commissioners, etc. discharged.

[Reproduced from *Seventeenth Century Economic Documents*, eds J. Thirsk and J.P. Cooper (Oxford University Press, 1972) pp. 162–4 by permission of the publishers and Dr Thirsk].

Appendix 3 (ii)

The Second Corn Bounty Act, 1688
(*Statutes at Large*, III, pp. 398–9 and *Pickering's Statutes* IX, pp. 14–15, 1 Will. & Mary, c. 12)

An act for the encouraging the exportation of corn.

FOrafmuch *as it hath been found by experience, that the exportation of corn and grain into foreign parts, when the price thereof is at a low rate in this kingdom, hath been a great advantage not only to the owners of land, but to the trade of this kingdom in general.*

Perfons exporting corn at fuch a rate fhall have a reward. Rates of corn. II. Be it therefore enacted by the King's and Queen's moft excellent majefties, by and with the advice and confent of the lords fpiritual and temporal, and of the commons, now affembled in parliament, and by the authority of the fame, That when malt or barley, *Winchefter* meafure, is or fhall be at four and twenty fhillings *per* quarter, or under ; rye at two and thirty fhillings *per* quarter, or under ; and wheat at eight and forty fhillings a quarter, or under, in any port or ports of this kingdom or dominion of *Wales*; every merchant or other perfon, who fhall put on fhip-board in *Englifh* fhipping, the mafter and two thirds of his mariners at leaft being their Majefties fubjects, any forts of the corn aforefaid, from any fuch ports where the rates fhall not then be higher than as aforefaid, with intent to export the faid corn to parts beyond the feas : Every fuch mer-**Exporter gives certificate of quantity, and bond to export.** chant or other perfon fhall bring a certificate in writing under his or their hands, containing the quantity and quality of corn fo fhipped, to the farmers, commiffioners, collectors, or other perfons appointed, or to be appointed, for the time being, to collect the duties and rates arifing by cuftoms within any fuch **See farther provifions relating hereto, 2 Geo. 2. c. 18.** port, and upon proof made of any fuch certificate by one or more credible perfon or perfons upon their oaths, which oaths the faid commiffioners or other perfons are hereby authorized and required to adminifter, and upon bond given by every fuch merchant, or other perfon, in the fum of two hundred pounds at the leaft for every hundred tons of corn fo fhipped, and fo proportionably, that the faid corn (danger of the feas excepted) fhall be exported into parts beyond the feas, and not be again landed in the kingdom of *England*, dominion of *Wales*, the iflands of *Guernfey* and *Jerfey*, or town of *Berwick* upon *Tweed* : **Reward paid to the exporter by the collectors.** Every fuch merchant fo fhipping off any of the aforefaid corn, and giving certificate and bond, as aforefaid, fhall have and receive from fuch farmers, commiffioners, collectors, or other perfons in any port refpectively, where the fame corn fhall be

farther pro-
ions as to
lt, by 5 Ann.
29. f. 15. &
fo fhipped, for every quarter of barley or malt, ground or unground, two fhillings and fix pence; for every quarter of rye,
ground or unground, three fhillings and fix pence; for every
quarter of wheat, ground or unground, five fhillings: Which 12 Annæ, ftat.
fum or fums every fuch commiffioner, farmer, or other perfon, 1. c. 2. f. 29.
are hereby authorized and required, upon demand by fuch exporter, to make prefent payment of accordingly, without taking
or requiring any thing for cuftom, or any fee or reward for corn
fo laden to be exported, or for fo much grain as fhall be exported, in any fhip wherein any other goods fhall be fhipped; any
law, ftatute, or ufage in any wife to the contrary notwithftand-
ing: And upon certificate returned under the common feal of Exporters
the chief magiftrate in any place or places beyond the feas, or bond how dif-
under the hands and feals of two known *Englifh* merchants up- charged.
Further pro-
on the place, that fuch corn was there landed, or upon proof by *vided for by*
credible perfons, that fuch corn was taken by enemies, or pe- 12 & 13 W. 3.
rifhed in the feas, the examination and proof thereof being left c. 10.
to the judgment of fuch commiffioners, farmers, collectors,
or other perfons; which proof being made, or certificate delivered to fuch perfon or perfons refpectively, as took bond, as
aforefaid, the faid bond fhall be delivered up to fuch importer
or his order, to be cancelled, without any fee for the fame: Collectors al-
And the monies by any fuch commiffioners, farmers, collectors, lowed the mo-
or other perfon, fo paid in obedience to this act, fhall be ac- ney in their
cepted of in his or their accounts, as fo much paid to their accounts.
Majefties, and he and they is and fhall be difcharged therefore
accordingly.

Appendix 3 (iii)

An Act for punishing such Persons as shall do Injuries and Violences to the Persons or Properties of his Majesty's Subjects, with Intent to hinder the Exportation of Corn, 1737
(*Statutes at Large* VI, pp. 71–2 and *Pickering's Statutes* XVII, pp. 194–7, 11 Geo. II, c. 22)

Preamble.

WHEREAS *many diforderly and evil-minded perfons have of late frequently affembled themfelves in great numbers, committed great violences, and done many injuries to the perfons and properties of his Majefty's fubjects, with intent to hinder the exportation of corn, whereby many of his Majefty's fubjects have been deterred from buying of corn and grain, and following their lawful bufinefs therein, to their great lofs and damage, as well as the great damage and prejudice of the farmers and landholders of this kingdom, and of the nation in general*; for the better preventing fuch wicked and diforderly practices, and more eafily and effectually bringing fuch offenders to condign punifhment, be it enacted by the King's moft excellent majefty, by and with the advice and confent of the lords fpiritual and temporal, and commons, in this prefent **Perfons ufing** parliament affembled, and by the authority of the fame, That **violence to** if any perfon or perfons fhall from and after the four and twen- **hinder the** tieth day of *June*, one thoufand feven hundred and thirty eight, **purchafe or** wilfully and malicioufly beat, wound, or ufe any other violence **carriage of** to or upon any perfon or perfons, with intent to deter or hinder **corn,** him or them from buying of corn or grain in any market or other place within this kingdom; or fhall unlawfully ftop or feize upon any waggon, cart or other carriage, or horfe, loaded with wheat, flour, meal, malt or other grain, in or on the way to or from any city, market town, or fea port of this kingdom, and wilfully and malicioufly break, cut, feparate, or deftroy the fame, or any part thereof, or the harnefs of the horfes drawing the fame; or fhall unlawfully take off, drive away, kill or wound any of fuch horfes, or unlawfully beat or wound the driver or drivers of fuch waggon, cart or other carriage, or horfe, fo loaded, in order to ftop the fame; or fhall, by cutting of the facks, or otherwife, fcatter or throw abroad fuch wheat, flour, meal, malt, or other grain, or fhall take or carry away, fpoil or damage the fame, or any part thereof; every and all fuch perfon and perfons being thereof lawfully convicted before any two or more juftices of the peace of the county, fhire, ftewartry, riding, divifion, town or place corporate, wherein fuch offence or offences fhall be committed, or before the juftices of the peace in open feffions (who are hereby authorized and impowered fummarily and finally to hear and determine the fame) fhall be fent to be imprifoned, to the common gaol, or to the houfe of correction, there to continue and be kept to hard labour for any time not exceeding the fpace of three months, nor lefs than one month; and fhall by and publickly the fame juftices be alfo ordered to be once publickly and openly whipped by the maffer or keeper of fuch gaol or houfe of correction, in fuch city, market town, or fea port, in or near to which fuch offence fhall be committed, on the firft convenient market day, at the market crofs or market place there, between the hours of eleven and two of the clock.

II. And be it further enacted by the authority aforefaid, That Committing if any fuch perfon or perfons fo convicted fhall commit any of the like offences aforefaid a fecond time; or if from and after the fences a fefaid four and twentieth day of *June*, one thoufand feven hundred and thirty eight, any perfon or perfons fhall wilfully and malicioufly pull, throw down, or otherwife deftroy any ftore- deftroying houfe or granary, or other place where corn fhall be then kept granaries of in order to be exported; or fhall unlawfully enter any fuch therein, ftorehoufe, granary, or other place, and take and carry away any corn, flour, meal, or grain therefrom, or fhall throw abroad or fpoil the fame, or any part thereof; or fhall unlawfully enter on board any fhip, barge, boat or veffel, and fhall wilfully and or in veffels, malicioufly take and carry away, caft, or throw out therefrom, &c. or otherwife fpoil or damage,, any meal, flour, wheat or grain therein intended for exportation; every perfon fo offending, and being thereof lawfully convicted, fhall be adjudged guilty of felony, and fhall be tranfported for the fpace of feven years, in Felony. like manner as other felons are directed to be tranfported by the laws and ftatutes of this realm; and if any fuch offender fo tranfported fhall return into this kingdom before the expiration of the faid feven years, he or fhe fhall fuffer death as a felon without benefit of clergy.

III. Provided always, That no attainder for any offence made Provifoes, felony by virtue of this act fhall make or work any corruption of blood, lofs of dower, or difinheritance of heir or heirs.

IV. Provided alfo, That no perfon who fhall be punifhed for any offence by virtue of this act, fhall be punifhed for the fame offence by virtue of any other law or ftatute whatfoever. Satisfaction

V. And be it further enacted by the authority aforefaid, That for fuch dafrom and after the four and twentieth day of *June*, one thou- mages recofand feven hundred and thirty eight, the inhabitants of every verable from hundred in that part of *Great Britain* called *England*, wherein the hundred, any fuch offence as aforefaid fhall be committed, fhall make

105

full fatisfaction and amends to all and every the perfon and perfons, their executors and adminiftrators, for the damages they
fhall have fuftained or fuffered by any injury or violence done to
their properties by any offender or offenders againft this act;
and that every perfon and perfons, who fhall fuftain damages in
their properties by any of the faid offences, fhall and are hereby
enabled to fue for and recover fuch his or their damages (the fum
(not exceed-
ing 100 l.)
to be recovered not exceeding one hundred pounds) againft the
faid hundred, who by this act fhall be made liable to anfwer all
or any part thereof; fuch damages to be fued for, levied, and
raifed, in fuch manner and form, and by and under the like
methods and directions, as are prefcribed and mentioned in
as in cafes of
robbery.
cafes of actions for robberies on the highway, in and by an act
made in the feven and twentieth year of the reign of Queen
Elizabeth, intituled, *An act for the following Hue and Cry*, and
by one other act made in the eighth year of the reign of his
prefent Majefty, intituled, *An act for the amendment of the laws
relating to the actions on the ftatute of Hue and Cry*, except fo
much thereof as relates to giving, leaving, or publifhing notice,
or making frefh fuit and hue and cry, or any other matter otherwife provided for by this act.

But notice is
to be given
within 2 days
after the fact
to a conftable:
VI. Provided neverthelefs, and be it further enacted by the
authority aforefaid, That no perfon or perfons fhall be enabled
to recover any damages by virtue of this act, unlefs he or they
by themfelves or by their fervants within two days after fuch
damage or injury done him or them by any fuch offender or
offenders as aforefaid, fhall give notice of fuch offence done and
committed to one of the conftables of the hundred, or to the
conftable, borfholder, headborough, or tythingman of the town,
parifh, village, hamlet, or tything, in or near which fuch fact
fhall be committed; and fhall, within ten days after fuch notice
and exami-
nation upon
oath within
10 days.
give in his or their examinations upon oath, or the examination
upon oath of his or their fervants being prefent at the time of
the fact being committed, or having the care of fuch his or their
properties, to which fuch damage or injury fhall be done, before
any juftice of the peace of the county, liberty, or divifion, where
fuch fact fhall be committed, whether he or they do know the
perfon or perfons that committed fuch fact, or any of them;
and if upon fuch examination it be confeffed, that he or they
do know the perfon or perfons that committed the faid fact, or
any of them; that then he or they fo confeffing fhall be bound
by recognizance to profecute fuch offender or offenders according to this act, or otherwife according to the laws of the
realm.

VII. Provided alſo, and be it enacted by the authority afore-

ſaid, That where any offence ſhall be committed againſt this act, and any one of the ſaid offenders ſhall be apprehended and lawfully convicted of ſuch offence within the ſpace of twelve months after the offence committed; no hundred, or franchiſe therein ſhall in any wiſe be ſubject or liable to make any ſatisfaction to the party or parties injured for the damages he or they ſhall have ſuſtained; any thing in this act contained to the contrary notwithſtanding.

VIII. Provided alſo, That no perſon who ſhall ſuſtain any damage by reaſon of any offence to be committed by any offender contrary to this act, ſhall be enabled hereby to ſue or bring any action againſt any hundred where ſuch offence ſhall be committed, till after the expiration of one year; nor unleſs the party or parties ſuſtaining ſuch damage, ſhall commence his, her, or their action or ſuit within two years next after the offence ſhall be committed.

Appendix 4 (i)

Commissioners of Customs and Excise: instructions to Collectors of Customs at the outports on the method to be observed in making allowance upon corn exported, 1731

(1)

The Method *to be observed in making the Allowance upon Corn exported, in purfuance of an Act of Parliament in the Firſt Year of the Reign of their Majeſties King* William *and* Queen Mary.

I. UPON the Signification of any Merchant of his Intentions to ſhip any *Malt, Rye, Barley,* or *Wheat,* ground or unground, for any Places beyond the Seas, in purſuance of the aforeſaid Act, the Collector and Comptroller being firſt ſatisfied by the Surveyor of the Act of Navigation, or his Deputy, that the Ship upon which the ſaid Corn is intended to be laden is a *Britiſh* built Ship, or a Foreign built Ship made free, and navigated as the Law directs, they are to grant a Sufferance under their Hands for the putting the ſame on board, which is to be directed to the Patent-Searcher, and alſo to the Surveyor and Land-Waiter of the Port, if any; and where there is no Surveyor or Land-Waiter, the Sufferance to be directed to the Patent-Searcher only.

II. THE ſaid Patent-Searcher, Surveyor and Land-Waiter, are to attend and diligently inſpect the lading of the ſaid Corn, that ſo they may ſee and be ſatisfied of the Meaſure and Quality thereof; and where there is no Surveyor or Land-Waiter, the Collector to ſee the Execution thereof with the Patent-Searcher; and the ſaid Officers are, in purſuance of the Act paſſed in the Second Year of King *GEORGE* the Second, to admeaſure all ſuch Corn, which may, for greater Expedition, be done by a Tub or Meaſure containing Four *Wincheſter* Buſhels; or if ſuch Corn or Grain is intended to be exported in Sacks, the ſaid Officers may make choice of Two of thoſe Sacks out of Twenty, and ſo in Proportion, before the ſame ſhall be put on board for Exportation, in order to compute the Quantity ſo intended to be ſhipp'd; and the Quantity and Quality of the Corn ſo ſhipp'd is forthwith to be endors'd upon the back of the Sufferance by all the Officers that affiſted at the lading thereof, and then to be return'd back to the Collector.

III. After the lading the ſaid *Rye, Barley* or *Wheat,* every Merchant, or other Perſon or Perſons exporting the ſame, are to bring a Certificate to the Collector in Writing under his or their Hands, containing the Quantity and Quality of the Corn ſo ſhipp'd, which he or they are to make farther Proof of by the Oath of one or more credible Perſons, whereupon the Collector is, with the Privity of the Comptroller, to take a Bond of the ſaid Perſon or Perſons ſo exporting, to bring a Certificate of the landing thereof beyond Sea; which being perform'd, a Cocquet is to be granted for the ſaid Corn in due Form, which is to be deliver'd to the Merchant, who is to endorſe the Quantity of Corn ſhipp'd on the back thereof;

108

before the Ship be clear'd Outwards. But as to *Malt*, the Merchant is to have Liberty to enter what Quantity he pleafes on board fuch Ship, and to give Bond for the Quantity fo enter'd, before he fhips any Part thereof, in the Conditions mentioned in the annexed Form of a Bond; and when fuch Bond is given, the Entry is to be delivered to the Searcher, who is to permit the Quantity of *Malt* fpecified in fuch Entry to be fhipp'd as it co res to hand; and, for the greater Expedition, fuch *Malt* may be meafured in the manner directed in the Second Article; and the Quantity of *Malt* fo fhipp'd is forthwith to be endorfed upon the back of the Entry by the Searcher, or his Deputy, and the Meeter that affifted at the lading thereof; and the Collector and Comptroller are to compare fuch Endorfement with the feveral Certificates granted by the Excife-Officers, containing an Account of the Quantity of *Barley* enter'd with them to be made into fuch *Malt*, and alfo the Quantity of *Malt* for which the Bounty is to be paid, reckoning Thirty Quarters of *Malt* to be the Produce of Twenty Quarters of *Barley*, in purfuance of the Acts paffed in the Third and Fourth Years of his prefent Majefty, which Certificates are to be produced to them before the clearing of the Ship; and if the difference is not confiderable, and no reafon to fufpect a Fraud, a Debenture may then be made out, annexing the Certificates to the Debenture, provided the other Requifites of Law are duly comply'd with. If the Merchant fhall intend to fhip more *Malt* than is exprefied in his firft Entry and Bond, he is before the fhipping thereof to make a fecond Entry, and give a further Bond in the fame manner as on his firft Entry; but if the Quantity of *Malt* fhipp'd fhall be lefs than is exprefied in the Entry or Bond, the Merchant himfelf is, agreeable to the Condition of his Bond, to endorfe the Quantity fhort fhipp'd, which is to be certified by the Searcher, or his Deputy.

IV. Before the Payment of the Money payable by the faid Acts for fuch Corn, the Patent-Searcher, as alfo the Surveyor and Land-Waiter, if any belong to the Port, are upon the faid Certificate or Debenture to atteft the Quantity and Quality of the Corn fo laden, and the Surveyor of the Act of Navigation, or his Deputy, is to atteft upon the Certificate the Qualification of the Ship, whether it be a *Britifh* built Ship, or a Foreign built Ship made free, and navigated with the Mafter and Two Thirds of the Mariners *Britifh*; which being perform'd, the Collector and Comptroller are to compute the Sums of Money which are due and payable for the fame, according to the faid Acts, which they are to enter upon the backfide of the Certificate or Debenture, and to atteft the fame under their Hands; and the Patent Officers are to take the Exporter's Oath that the faid Corn, both for Quantity and Quality, fo fhipp'd, was really exported into Parts beyond the Seas, and not again landed in *Great-Britain*, the Iflands of *Guernfey* or *Jerfey*, or Town of *Berwick*.

V. Upon the Payment of the Money, the Collector is to take the Merchant's Acquittance upon the faid Certificate or Debenture for the fame, and no Fee is to be taken from the Merchant for any Matter relating to the faid Act.

VI. The Collector is not to deliver up any fuch Bond before a Certificate be brought under the common Seal of the chief Magiftrate in any Place or Places beyond the Seas, or under the Hands and Seals of Two known *Britifh* Merchants upon the Place, that fuch Corn was there landed, and Proof by credible Perfons that fuch Corn was taken by Enemies or perifh'd in the Seas, as the faid Law directs; and the Collector and Comptroller are carefully and diligently to examine the Truth and Reality of fuch Certificates, and the Credit and Value of the Perfons certifying, before fuch Bond be delivered up.

VII. The Collector is to take care and to give Direction to all the Officers of the Port, to have a watchful Eye that none of the faid Sorts of Corn fhipped to be carried beyond the Seas, in order to receive the faid Allowance, be landed again in that Port, nor carried to any other Port of *Great-Britain*; and he is daily to inform himfelf of all Sorts of Corn that are brought into his Port by Coaft-Cocquet

109

or *Tranfire*, or otherwife, from any other Port of *Great-Britain*, that fo no Corn for which the faid Allowance hath been granted in any other Port, be there landed.

VIII. If any Sort of Corn or Grain, except *Malt*, *Barley*, *Wheat* or *Rye*, be exported, as *Oats*, *Peafe*, *Buckwheat*, *Beans*, &c. they are not to have the Allowance; and if any Corn be fhipped upon any other Shipping than *Britifh* Shipping, or not navigated according to Law, or Proof not made as the Law directs, the Collector is not to make any Allowance.

Exceptions ag.t the Bounty.

IX. And whereas the Allowance upon *Malt*, *Barley*, *Rye* and *Wheat*, are not to be made but when the faid feveral Sorts of Corn are under the Rates mention'd in the aforefaid Law, if at any time the Collector fhall have reafon to fufpect and believe the Prices thereof refpectively are above the Rates mention'd in the faid Act, he is, before he allows of any Certificate brought by any Perfon concerning the Price of fuch Corn, to examine the real Price; and in cafe of any Doubt, to reprefent the fame to the Commiffioners, for farther Directions thereupon.

Terms for Allowance Bounty.

X. In cafe any *Wheat*, *Rye*, *Barley* or *Malt*, ground or unground, fhall be exported for the Ufe of any of his Majefty's Garifons, or fhipp'd on board any Ships bound for *Newfoundland*, or any other Place, for brewing of Beer or baking of Bread for the Voyage, no Bounty is to be allow'd for the fame.

Exceptions

This Article ftruck out by Secretarys L 20 April 17

XI. And whereas fuch as are to have their Allowances given by the foremention'd Act, are thereby directed to fhip the faid Sorts of Corn and Grain from fuch Ports where they demand the faid Allowance, and to bring a Certificate that the fame was fo fhipp'd to the Collector of fuch Port, no Allowance is to be made by the Collector for any Corn not fhipp'd in your Port.

Do.

XII. The fame Rules (except fuch as relates to *Malt*) are to be obferved in the examining and fhipping *Bear*, alias *Bigg*, *Oatmeal*, and *Malt* made of *Wheat*, or *Wheat-malt*, whereon there is a Bounty, intended for Exportation.

Do.

XIII. When it fhall happen that the Collector has not Money fufficient in his Hands to pay any Corn-Debentures, a Certificate of the want of Money to pay the fame is to be made, and a Duplicate, or an Account thereof, fent to the Board, according to the Form under mention'd, to be compar'd with the Debenture when produced to the Commiffioners for Payment, agreeable to the Order dated the 31ft of *May*, 1718, viz.

Colle.

Date.	Exporter's Name.	Ship.	Mafter's Name.	Whither bound.	Species.	Bounty. *l. s. d.*

Cuftom-Houfe, *London*.

19 Febry 1731

By Order of the Commiffioners.

Appendix 4 (ii)

Commissioners of Customs: bond for malt exported, 1731

*N*OVerint Univerfi per præfentes, Nos

teneri & firmiter obligari Sereniffimo Domino noftro Georgio
Secundo, Dei Gratia, Magnæ Britanniæ, Franciæ & Hiberniæ,
Regi, *Fidei Defenfor,* &c. *in*

*Libris bonæ & legalis Monetæ, folvend'
eidem Domino Regi, Hæredibus vel Executoribus fuis : Ad
quam quidem folutionem bene & fideliter faciend' obligamus
Nos   per fe,
pro toto, & in folido, Hæredes, Executores & Adminiftratores
noftros, & cujuflibet noftrum, firmiter per præfentes. Sigillis
noftris figillat. Dat'*   *die*   *Anno
Regni Regis prædict'* &c.   *Annoque
Domini* 173

W HER EAS the above bounden
                          hath this Day entred for Exportation
              with the Collector of his Majefty's Cuftoms in the Port
of   to be fhipp'd on board the
                          whereof
is Mafter, now riding at anchor, and bound for
                              Quarters and
              of Malt.

Now the Condition of this Obligation is fuch, That if the faid
                              Quarters and
              of Malt, and every Part thereof (except fo
much thereof as fhall be endorfed on the back of this Bond by the
above bounden

and certified by the Searcher not to have been shipp'd) shall be exported into Parts beyond the Seas (the Danger of the Seas excepted) and that the said Malt, or any Part thereof, shall not be landed again in *Great-Britain*, or in the Islands of *Guernsey* or *Jersey*, then this Obligation shall be void, and of none effect, or else to remain in full Force and Virtue.

*Sealed and delivered
in the Presence of*

Notes

I Primitive Accumulation and the Problem of Agrarian Capitalism

1. E. J. Hobsbawm, 'Perry Anderson's History', author's transcript of a (tape-recorded) lecture given at the University of Kent, Canterbury, May 1976, p. 14.
2. On 'productivist Marxism' as discussed by Communist Party historians, see R. Samuel, 'British Marxist Historians, 1880–1980', Part One, *New Left Review* 120 (1980) pp. 81–3.
3. M. Dobb, *Studies in the Development of Capitalism* (1946) provided the point of departure. Criticisms of Dobb's book were originally published in the journal *Science and Society*, and these have been gathered together and augmented in R. H. Hilton (ed.), *The Transition from Feudalism to Capitalism* (1976); see also R. Brenner, 'The Origins of Capitalist Development: a critique of Neo-Smithian Marxism', *New Left Review* 104 (1977) pp. 25–92.
4. See D. J. Ormrod, 'R. H. Tawney and the Origins of Capitalism', *History Workshop Journal*, 18 (1984) pp. 147–9.
5. J. P. Cooper pointed out that Brenner 'joins a long line of expositors beginning with the Physiocrats' ('In Search of Agrarian Capitalism', *Past and Present* 80 (1978) p. 20, discussing Brenner's 'Agrarian Class Structure and Economic Development in Pre-Industrial Europe', *Past and Present* 70 (1976) pp. 30–75.)
6. A. Smith, *An Inquiry into the Nature and Causes of the Wealth of Nations* (1776; ed. J. R. McCulloch, 1838) pp. 170–87.
7. K. Marx, *Theories of Surplus Value* (1862; repr. Lawrence and Wishart, 1951) p. 44.
8. Cooper, 'In Search of Agrarian Capitalism', pp. 27, 29.
9. Marx, *Theories of Surplus Value*, pp. 44–104. Marx, *Grundrisse* (1857/8; Pelican ed., 1973) p. 508, 'Monetary wealth – as merchant wealth – had admittedly helped to speed up and to dissolve the old relations of production, and made it possible for the proprietor of land for example, as A. Smith already nicely develops, to exchange his grain and cattle etc. for use values brought from afar, instead of squandering the use values he himself produced, along with his retainers, and to locate his wealth in great part in the mass of his co-consuming retainers.'
10. Marx, *Capital*, vol. I (1954, Moscow ed.) p. 721.
11. Ibid., p. 714.
12. Marx, *Capital*, vol. III (1959, Moscow ed.) p. 320.
13. L. Althusser, *Lenin and Philosophy* (1971) p. 90; B. Hindess and P. Hirst, *Pre-Capitalist Modes of Production* (1974) p. 288.
14. G. Bois, 'Against the Neo-Malthusian Orthodoxy', *Past and Present* 79 (1978) p. 67, 'In fact, the result of Professor Brenner's approach is to deprive the basic concept of historical materialism, that is the mode of production, of all real substance'.
15. P. Croot and D. Parker, 'Agrarian Class Structure and Economic Development in Pre-Industrial Europe', *Past and Present* 78 (1978) p. 39.

16. H. J. Habakkuk, 'La disparition du paysan anglais', *Annales ESC* XX (1965) especially pp. 655–63; J. Saville, 'Primitive Accumulation and Early Industrialization in Britain', *Socialist Register* (1969) pp. 251, 263; G. E. Mingay, *Enclosure and the Small Farmer in the Age of the Industrial Revolution* (1968) pp. 31–2.

17. J. Thirsk, 'Enclosing and Engrossing', chapter IV in J. Thirsk (ed.), *The Agrarian History of England and Wales*, vol. IV: *1500–1640* (1967) pp. 200–55.

18. Ibid., p. 228.

19. Brenner adds a further element of polarisation by discussing the respective arguments of Sweezy and Dobb in two separate articles in different journals, namely, 'The Origins of Capitalist Development: a critique of Neo-Smithian Marxism', *New Left Review* 104 (1977), which mainly discusses the ideas of Sweezy, Frank and Wallerstein, and 'Dobb on the Transition from Feudalism to Capitalism', *Cambridge Journal of Economics* 2 (1978). Sweezy has claimed that he and Dobb were in close agreement on the rise of capitalism, especially on commodity circulation and Marx's contention that 'The circulation of commodities is the starting point of capital. Commodity production, *trade*, form *the historical preconditions* under which it arises. World trade and the world market open up in the sixteenth century the modern life history of capital', P. Sweezy, 'Communications – Comment on Brenner [on the origins of capitalist development]', *New Left Review* 108 (1978) pp. 94–5. Sweezy reiterates the point made above that it is essential to distinguish analytically and chronologically, between the decline of feudalism and the rise of capitalism, as Dobb in fact did.

20. R. H. Tawney, *The Agrarian Problem in the Sixteenth Century* (1912) p. 3: 'The agrarian changes of the sixteenth century may be regarded as a long step in the commercialisation of English life. The growth of the textile industries is closely connected with the development of pasture farming, and it was the export of woollen cloth, that "prodigy of trade", which first brought England conspicuously into world commerce, and was the motive for more than one of those early expeditions to discover new markets, out of which grew plantations, colonies, and empire.'

21. M. A. Havinden, review of E. Kerridge (ed.), *Agrarian Problems in the Sixteenth Century and After* (1969), in the *Agricultural History Review* XIX (1971) p. 181. Tawney wrote, 'Landholding tends, in short, to become commercialised' and 'The command of money was now more important than the command of men', *The Agrarian Problem*, p. 187.

22. E. Kerridge, 'The Movement of Rent, 1540–1640', *Econ. Hist. Rev.*, 2nd ser. VI (1953).

23. Dobb, *Studies*, p. 123, quoting Marx, *Capital*, vol. III, pp. 388–96. The main thesis of Unwin's *Studies in Industrial Organisation in the Sixteenth and Seventeenth Centuries* (1904), came to light in 1900 as a result of intensive archival work on the smaller London companies. He described his discovery in his diary, 25 May 1900: 'There is the liberal free-trade merchant class, whose capital was coming to control industry, and who supported the Parliament. And, on the other hand, there are the small trader and handicraftsman struggling for economic independence, and this class the king had every desire to conciliate.' The close parallel with Marx's 'two paths' is very striking though Unwin was apparently unaware of this, and his work was based entirely on his pioneering use of the unpublished records of the City Companies. Its importance is discussed by Tawney in his introductory Memoir in R. H. Tawney (ed.), *Studies in Economic History: the collected papers of George Unwin* (1927) pp. xxxviii–xxxix. It was largely on the basis of Unwin's work that Dobb argued that there were 'two decisive moments' in the history of capitalism in England, the first in the early seventeenth century centring on the struggle within the chartered corporations and the parliamentary struggle against monopoly, and the second, the industrial revolution [Dobb, *Studies*, pp. 18–19].

24. Dobb, *Studies*, p. 26.
25. Ibid., p. 17.
26. P. H. Aron, 'M. N. Pokrovskii and the Impact of the First Five-Year Plan on Soviet Historiography', in J. S. Curtiss (ed.), *Essays in Russian and Soviet Historiography* (1963) pp. 290–2; see also J. Barber, 'The Establishment of Intellectual Orthodoxy in the U.S.S.R., 1928–1934', *Past and Present* 83 (1979) pp. 158–9.
27. E. J. Hobsbawm, 'The Historians' Group of the Communist Party', in M. Cornforth (ed.), *Rebels and their Causes: essays in honour of A. L. Morton* (1978) p. 32.
28. M. Dobb, 'The Transition from Feudalism to Capitalism', *Science and Society* XXVII (1964) and reprinted in M. Dobb, *Papers on Capitalism, Development and Planning* (1967) pp. 15–16.
29. H. Medick, 'The Proto-industrial Family Economy: the structural function of household and family during the transition from peasant society to industrial capitalism', *Social History* 3 (1976) p. 296; P. Kriedte, H. Medick and J. Schlumbohm, *Industrialisation before Industrialisation: rural industry in the genesis of capitalism* (Cambridge, 1981).
30. B. E. Supple, *Commercial Crisis and Change in England, 1600–1642* (Cambridge, 1959).
31. J. U. Nef, 'The Progress of Technology and the Growth of Large-Scale Industry in Great Britain, 1540–1640', *Econ. Hist. Rev.* V (1934–5); D. C. Coleman, 'Industrial Growth and Industrial Revolutions', *Economica*, n.s. XXIII (1956); S. M. Jack, *Trade and Industry in Tudor and Stuart England* (1977).
32. E. L. Jones, 'The Agricultural Origins of Industry', *Past and Present* 40 (1968); J. Thirsk, 'Industries in the Countryside' in F. J. Fisher (ed.), *Essays in the Economic and Social History of Tudor and Stuart England* (Cambridge, 1961).
33. Medick, 'Proto-industrial Family Economy', p. 297.
34. Supple, *Commercial Crisis and Change*, chapter 3.
35. Medick, 'Proto-industrial Family Economy', p. 299.
36. Ibid., pp. 299–300.
37. Dobb, 'From Feudalism to Capitalism', *Marxism Today* (Sept. 1962), reprinted in Hilton, *The Transition from Feudalism to Capitalism*, p. 167. Dobb repeatedly emphasised this point, both in the *Studies* and in subsequent discussion.
38. E. Hazelkorn, 'Some Problems with Marx's Theory of Capitalist Penetration into Agriculture: the case of Ireland', *Economy and Society* 10 (1981) p. 292.
39. E. J. Hobsbawm, 'Capitalisme et Agriculture: les Réformateurs Écossais au XVIIIe Siècle', *Annales ESC* 3 (1978) p. 582.
40. Sir J. Steuart, *An Inquiry into the Principles of Political Oeconomy* (1767; ed. A. S. Skinner in two vols, Edinburgh and London, 1966).
41. A. J. Youngson, *After the Forty-Five: the economic impact on the Scottish Highlands* (Edinburgh, 1973) p. 62.
42. S. R. Sen, *The Economics of Sir James Steuart* (1957) p. 2.
43. K. Marx, *Theories of Surplus Value*, pp. 42–3.
44. Steuart, *Principles*, vol. I, pp. 59–66, 105–10.
45. Ibid., p. 59.
46. Ibid., p. 108.
47. Ibid., pp. 64–5.
48. K. Kautsky, *Die agrarfrage* (Stuttgart, 1899), quoted by Hazelkorn, 'Marx's Theory of Capitalist Penetration into Agriculture', p. 301.
49. E. J. Hobsbawm, 'Perry Anderson's History', p. 23. See footnote 1.
50. F. J. Fisher, 'The Development of the London Food Market, 1540–1640', *Econ. Hist. Rev.* V (1935); E. A. Wrigley, 'A Simple Model of London's Importance in a Changing English Society and Economy, 1650–1750', *Past and Present* 37 (1967).

51. D. J. Ormrod, 'Dutch Commercial and Industrial Decline and British Growth in the late Seventeenth and Early Eighteenth Centuries' in F. Krantz and P. Hohenberg, *Failed Transitions to Modern Industrial Society: Renaissance Italy and Seventeenth Century Holland* (Montreal, 1974) pp. 36–43.

52. Tawney, *Agrarian Problem*, pp. 177–310; Thirsk, *Agrarian History of England and Wales*, pp. 200–55.

53. See especially Cooper, 'In Search of Agrarian Capitalism', which argues that in terms of organisation and levels of production, the divergence between French and English agriculture came between 1670 and 1720, p. 59.

54. G. E. Mingay, *Enclosure and the Small Farmer in the Age of the Industrial Revolution* (1968) p. 29; Saville, 'Primitive Accumulation', p. 254.

55. R. B. Outhwaite, 'Food Crises in Early Modern England: patterns of public response', in *Proceedings of the Seventh International Economic History Congress*, vol. 2, ed. M. Flinn (Edinburgh, 1978) p. 370.

56. Proverbs, xi: 26.

57. The phrase is Heckscher's, see E. F. Heckscher, *Mercantilism* (1931) vol. II, Part III, chapter III, pp. 80–111.

58. D. G. Barnes, *History of the English Corn Laws* (1930) pp. 23–33; also see below, pp. 86–90.

59. British Library of Political and Economic Science, Tawney Papers, 1/8, p. 21; 4/1, p. 36.

60. R. B. Outhwaite, 'Food Crises in Early Modern England', p. 372.

61. Idem, 'Dearth and Government Intervention in English Grain Markets, 1590–1700', *Econ. Hist. Rev.*, 2nd ser. XXXIV (1981) pp. 396, 405–6.

62. A. B. Appleby, 'Grain Prices and Subsistence Crises in England and France, 1590–1740', *Journal of Economic History* 39 (1979).

63. Barnes, *English Corn Laws*, Appendix B, p. 297.

64. Ibid., p. 11; although Adam Smith argued that it served mainly commercial interests.

65. See Barnes, *English Corn Laws*, Appendix A for a list of statutes regulating the grain trade, based on H. Thornton, *Historical Summary of the Corn Laws* (1841).

66. Printed in J. Thirsk and J. P. Cooper (eds.), *Seventeenth-Century Economic Documents* (Oxford, 1972) p. 163.

67. For a very suggestive discussion, see E. P. Thompson 'The Moral Economy of the English Crowd in the Eighteenth Century', *Past and Present* 50 (1971) pp. 76–136.

68. Hindess and Hirst, *Pre-Capitalist Modes of Production* pp. 295, 297.

69. Arthur Young's arguments may be taken as being typical of those defending the bounty policy, e.g. *The Expediency of a Free Exportation of Corn at this Time* (1770) summarised by Barnes, *English Corn Laws*, pp. 27–8.

70. Ms notes by William Temple of Trowbridge in George Chalmers' copy of M. Combrune, *An Enquiry into the Prices of Wheat, Malt, and occasionally of Other Provisions* (1768) Goldsmith's Library, London.

71. 11 Geo. II, c. 22 (1737). See Appendix 3 (iii).

72. R. E. Prothero, *English Farming Past and Present* (1912; rev. ed. 1917) pp. 253, 255.

73. T. S. Ashton, *An Economic History of England: the 18th century* (1955) p. 48.

74. For a fairly typical example of this commonly-held view, see the *Gentleman's Magazine* (1752) (Extract of a letter from the *General Evening Post*, 25 Aug 1752):

'Tis by the bounty alone that we are enabled to supply foreign markets as cheap as other corn countries do; without it we should not have sold near so much to the French even this year; for I very well know they have purchased large quantities elsewhere, and at cheaper rates. 'Tis by the bounty alone that our hands are improved, and so valuable a trade is gained to the kingdom, by which we are become, as it were, the chief granary of Europe, and by which so many millions of money have been brought into the nation, and the value of our lands so much increased.

75. Brenner, 'Agrarian Class Structure', p. 68. The same view is reaffirmed, indeed it is transformed into a major conclusion and resolution of several arguments, in Brenner's rejoinder to his critics, 'The Agrarian Roots of European Capitalism', *Past and Present* 97 (1982) p. 113.

76. Cooper, 'In Search of Agrarian Capitalism', p. 53.

77. See especially A. H. John, 'The Course of Agricultural Change, 1660–1760', in L. S. Pressnell (ed.), *Studies in the Industrial Revolution: essays presented to T. S. Ashton* (1960) pp. 125–55; 'Aspects of English Economic Growth in the First Half of the Eighteenth Century', *Economica*, n.s., XXVIII (1961); 'Agricultural Productivity and Economic Growth in England, 1700–1760', *Journal of Economic History* XXV (1965).

78. A. H. John, 'English Agricultural Improvement and Grain Exports, 1660–1765', in D. C. Coleman and A. H. John (eds), *Trade, Government and Economy in Pre-Industrial England: essays presented to F. J. Fisher* (1976) pp. 45–67.

79. Personal communication, 4 October 1982, and an unpublished paper, 'The Political Consequences of the Eighteenth Century Grain Trade' by Dr J. M. Black (University of Durham).

80. See E. P. Thompson's criticism of P. Anderson and T. Nairn in 'The Peculiarities of the English' (1965), reprinted in E. P. Thompson (ed.), *The Poverty of Theory and Other Essays* (1978) p. 40: 'Despite disclaimers, neither Anderson nor Nairn appear to be able to accept, *au fond*, the notion of an agrarian class . . . as a true bourgeoisie.'

81. Steuart, *Inquiry*, vol. I, p. 118.

82. Ibid., pp. 30–3, 34–8; but the argument is linked with the extent to which 'a spirit of industry' takes root, that is to say, a low leisure-preference.

83. Ibid., pp. 110–16.

84. Ibid., p. 188.

85. Ibid., p. 103.

86. E. P. Thompson, 'Peculiarities of the English', p. 44.

II The Grain Trade anatomised, 1700–1760

1. 'A General View of the Corn Trade and Corn Laws of Great Britain', in the *Farmers' Magazine* XI (1802) pp. 277–96. In addition to the *General View of the Agriculture of Aberdeenshire* (1811), Skene Keith was the author of several tracts on agricultural subjects, currency, and demographic questions.

2. Keith, 'A General View of the Corn Trade', pp. 278–81.

3. Given the wide extent of annual fluctuations in the grain trade, depending largely on the state of the harvest, objection can legitimately be made against the use of a moving average. It has been undertaken however in order to facilitate visual comparison of various sets of figures, and because the trade can arguably be seen as a regular trade supplied by a growing surplus. But the trends shown in figures 1–3 should be read in conjunction with the annual grain export figures given in Appendix 1, pp. 96–7.

4. Customs House, London, Customs 97/1–16 (Yarmouth, Collector-Board). By 1744,

complaints begin to appear on this score together with requests for additional officers. The swollen amount of business at Yarmouth, for example, in the late 1740s and early 1750s is reflected in the changed format of the hitherto ill-kept port books; between 1746 and 1750, extended lateral entries were replaced by entries in four parallel columns for wheat, barley, malt and rye, (PRO: E. 190 557/8 (1746) and 558/13 (1750); books for the intervening years are missing). By this time, grain shipments were of overwhelming predominance in Yarmouth's export trade.

5. In January 1743, it was reported that, 'Three vessels laded with corn at Ipswich for Holland, were lately stopped in suspicion of false entries, and upon remeasuring the corn, 300 qrs were deficient, which was about a sixth of the whole: by this rule above £30,000 might be fraudulently got in one year.' *Gentleman's Magazine* XIII (1743) p. 49.

6. Perhaps because he omitted the word 'malt' from his own tables, although the figures for malt are included in his totals.

7. C. Davenant, 'A Second Report to the Commissioners for Stating the Public Accounts', 1711, in C. Whitworth (ed.), *The Political and Commercial Works of . . . Charles Davenant* V (1771) p. 426.

8. D. Defoe, *A Plan of the English Commerce* (1728) p. 234.

9. Barnes, *English Corn Laws,* p. 46, note 24 (quotation from the Townshend Papers, 1751).

10. PRO: C.O. 388/95, 'Particulars of the Trade carried on between the different Ports of his Majesty's Dominions and Rotterdam, and the other Ports of the Maas, and vice-versa', by Richard Wolters, Agent at Rotterdam, 16 July 1765, unpaginated. (Henceforth referred to as Consular Reports, Rotterdam, 1765).

11. NRO: Z.C.E. 10/12, Carr Ellison Mss R. Carr to T. M. Liebenrood, 29 Sept. 1739.

12. Spain, Portugal, and the Straits of Gibraltar received on average 51 per cent of English exports of wheat, rye, and oatmeal during the period 1749–51 as compared to Holland's 20 per cent; during the period 1744–6, the respective figures were 15 per cent and 39 per cent, (BL: Add. Ms 38387 ff. 31–52). On the course and organisation of the grain trade to Portugal, see H. E. S. Fisher, *The Portugal Trade* (1971) pp. 64–71, 115–16.

13. The East Anglian ports handled over three-quarters of total malt and barley exports during much of the period, see Table 4; see also Defoe, *Plan of the English Commerce*, p. 236, and O. Burrish, *Batavia Illustrata* (1728) p. 373.

14. M. Combrune, *An Enquiry into the Prices of Wheat, Malt, and Occasionally of Other Provisions* (1768) pp. 95–6.

15. By Sir Robert Southwell in a paper read before the Royal Society in 1675, and referred to in T. S. Willan, *The English Coasting Trade, 1600–1750* (Manchester, 1938) pp. xiv–xv.

16. C. Visser, *Verkeersindustrieen te Rotterdam in de tweede helft der Achttiende Eeuw* (Rotterdam, 1927) p. 97.

17. 1 Will. & Mary, c. 12.

18. With the exception that all malt made from wheat was to receive a bounty of 5 s per quarter from 1 May 1707, by 5 Ann c. 29; Barnes, *English Corn Laws*, pp. 42–3.

19. 9 Will. III, c. 12; the duty was halved in 1725 by 11 Geo. I, c. 4.

20. 12 Geo. I, c. 4.

21. Burrish, *Batavia Illustrata*, p. 376.

22. For details of the malting process, see P. Mathias, *The Brewing Industry in England, 1700–1830* (Cambridge, 1959) pp. 406–11. The basic processes were these: after steeping in a cistern for three to four days, the water was drained off, and the barley was placed in a wooden 'couch' for twenty-four hours when swelling took place. It was then spread on the malthouse floor for germination, for twelve to fifteen days. According to the type of

malt being produced, the shoot of the grain (the 'acrospire') was allowed to grow to varying lengths, and vigorous 'acrospiring' could be encouraged by sprinkling with water. Finally, the germinated grain was dried on the kiln.

23. Custom House, London, Customs 48/11 (Excise and Treasury), 9 Nov. 1717. See also Mathias, *Brewing Industry*, p. 431.

24. Customs 48/11, loc. cit. These practices were perhaps facilitated by the fact that bounties were payable in London as well as the port of export. At Yarmouth in 1733 for example, £3134 of bounty money was paid at the port itself, while the remaining £17,001 was certified for payment in London (Customs 97/8, 4 Jan 1734).

25. Customs 48/11, 8 Dec. 1719.

26. By the early eighteenth century, it had become a common practice for brewers to undertake their own malting; but malt produced for the export trade generally used poorer quality barley than that produced by or for the inland trade. See below, p. 30.

27. W. T. Comber, *An Inquiry into the State of National Subsistence* (1808) pp. 142–3; M. Combrune, *Enquiry*, pp. 83–4.

28. Customs 48/11, loc. cit.

29. Mathias, *Brewing Industry*, pp. 408, 430. Malt with a long 'acrospire' was commonly described as 'long malt'.

30. Customs 97/3, 27 Oct. 1714.

31. Ibid.; see also Customs 97/5, 12 Sept. 1726, when samples were again taken of malt intended for Holland which was said to be 'little better than screening of malt . . . the officers seeing the corn rise badly out of the lighter . . . stopped the shipping that part which was very bad and lay at the bottom of the lighter.'

32. Visser, *Verkeersindustrieen*, p. 93; Lord Kinross, *The Kindred Spirit, a History of Gin and the House of Booth* (1959), p. 1.

33. Combrune, *Enquiry*, p. 68. The Excise Office acknowledged that 'Distillers in Holland can make spirits much cheaper than the distillers here can do', on account of the cheapness of English malt, although this was inconsistent with its basic argument that the malt export trade was of 'little or no value' (Customs 48/11, 9 Nov. 1717).

34. Burrish, *Batavia Illustrata*, p. 376.

35. Customs 48/11, 8 Dec. 1719; see also Customs 97/11, 1 Mar. 1741; Customs 97/2, 31 Oct. 1740; and Mathias, *Brewing Industry*, pp. 405, 408.

36. That is, whenever the drawback claimed exceeded the original amount of duty paid, or when unmalted was mixed with malted grain, and the malt bounty claimed for the whole amount.

37. 6 Geo. I, c. 21, taking effect from 1 June 1720. A draft appears in Customs 48/11, 5 Jan. 1720.

38. From 24 June 1726 by 12 Geo. I, c. 4. Maltsters intending to produce malt for export were in future obliged to give written notice before steeping began.

39. E.g. Customs 97/7, 25 Aug. 1731 concerning Robert Jarvis exporting malt to Rotterdam: '[The Excise Officers] are directed to take the measure of all malt made for exportation from the kiln and from thence the computation is made and entered into the books of how much malt made and barley steeped and the allowance of how much money the merchant is entitled to on exporting the malt produced from the barley so steeped is then settled. Sometimes the merchant ships his malt directly from the kiln but laid up in warehouses and the merchant ships as he has opportunity and will oftentimes take out more than the certificates mention as the stowage of his vessel requires, and sometimes less, by which custom a very considerable difference will arise at the clearing the storehouse between the excise certificates and our meters account for the last quantity shipped from the warehouse.'

40. Customs 97/9, 31 Dec. 1735.

41. Allowances were made for breaking during transport so that an exact balance was not required, ibid., 7 Feb. 1734.

42. By 3 Geo. II, c. 7, taking effect from 24 June 1730: 'For every twenty quarters of barley or other corn or grain that shall be entered and made into malt for exportation, an allowance of thirty quarters, after the same shall be dried and made into malt, and no more.'

43. In fact the Collector of Customs at Yarmouth thought that 'if the exporter is to have an allowance of thirty when his twenty quarters of barley made but twenty five quarters of malt, that such an allowance will open a door for great frauds for then they will make their malt fit for the home consumption and will ship it as for exportation, but will find ways to reland it or unship it at sea and send it to London when it is very easy to detect the fraud, by which they will save the duty and gain the allowance as though exported.' (Customs 97/6, 31 July 1730); Customs 97/11, 18 Nov. 1738; Ibid., 1 Mar. 1741.

44. Consular Reports, Rotterdam, 1765.

III Commercial Organisation

1. Mathias, *Brewing Industry*, pp. 465–6.

2. NNRO: Ms 6360/6B/8: Copy of all letters sent beyond the seas by Thomas Baret, Horshead, Nr. Norwich. Thomas Baret to Josiah Child, 5 Apr. 1695.

3. Customs 97/10, 11 Nov. 1737.

4. Customs 97/6, 21 Sept. 1730; Customs 97/3, 31 Dec. 1735.

5. Customs 48/15, 10 Feb. 1758.

6. Customs 97/3, 25 Aug. 1731.

7. PRO: E. 190, loc. cit.

8. H. Phillips, *The Thames about 1750* (1951) p. 39.

9. D. A. Baker, 'The Marketing of Corn in the First Half of the Eighteenth Century: North-East Kent', *Agricultural History Review* 18 (1970) pp. 126–50.

10. HUL: Ms D.P./82, Maister Ledger, entries for 12 Nov. 1714, 17 Dec. 1714, 15 and 18 Mar. 1715.

11. Maister Letters, consulted by kind permission of the late Col. R. A. Alec-Smith, Winestead, Hull.

12. NRO: Z.C.E. 10/11, R. Carr to J. G. Liebenrood, London 2 Nov. 1738.

13. Maister Letters, N. Maister to H. Maister, London, 13 Feb. 1738; N. Maister to H. Maister, London, ? Mar. 1738.

14. HUL: Ms D.P./82, Maister Ledger, loc. cit.

15. Maister Letters, N. Maister to H. Maister, London, 13 and 15 Feb. 1738.

16. NRO: Z.C.E. 10/11, R. Carr to Wm. Norton, Dunkirk, 20 Oct. 1738.

17. NRO: Z.C.E. 10/12, R. Carr to J. A. Crop, Amsterdam, 7 Aug. 1739; R. Carr to T. M. Liebenrood, Rotterdam, 14 Oct. 1739.

18. NRO: Z.C.E. 10/11, R. Carr to R. Hayes, Konigsberg, 2 Nov. 1738.

19. Customs 85/2 (Sunderland, Collector-Board), 13 June 1740.

20. PRO: 30/8 (Chatham Papers), 81, f. 187 (undated).

21. W. Forbes, *Memoirs of a Banking-House* (compiled 1803, publ. Edinburgh, 1859) p. 7.

22. Ibid., p. 12; GAA: Brants 1337, Letters of John Coutts & Comp., Edinburgh, and Coutts Bros. & Comp., Edinburgh, 1748–9 and 1755–8.

23. NRO: Z.C.E. 10/11–17; G. Jackson, *Hull in the Eighteenth Century* (1972) pp. 28, 31, 52.
24. D. J. Ormrod, 'Anglo-Dutch Commerce, 1700–1760' (University of Cambridge Ph.D. thesis, 1973) pp. 236–9.
25. GAR: N. Arch. 2332/74 A. I. & Z. Hope and B. Lowes, 25 Mar. 1738; see also ibid., 2332/43 24 Feb. 1738; 2328/657 28 Sept. 1734; 2345/350 25 Aug. 1750.
26. NRO: Z.C.E. 10/12, R. Carr to Wm. Norton, Dunkirk, 24 Apr. 1740. Exporting still continued in spite of scarcity and high prices at home. Later in the year, an embargo was laid but this failed to prevent export and the buying of grain for the export trade, as Carr explained: 'Notwithstanding the embargo upon corn, I find some people have exported for which they will be called to an account. Some ships are already seized in the So[und].' (Z.C.E. 10/13, R. Carr to T. M. Liebenrood, Rotterdam, 23 Jan. 1741). The Sound Toll Registers show that English grain was indeed shipped to Sweden during times of embargo, H. S. K. Kent, *War and Trade in Northern Seas: Anglo-Scandinavian economic relations in the mid-eighteenth century* (Cambridge, 1973) p. 96.
27. NRO: Z.C.E. 10/12, R. Carr to T. M. Liebenrood, Rotterdam, 11 May 1738.
28. Ibid., R. Carr to T. M. Liebenrood, Rotterdam, 5 June 1739.
29. NRO: Z.C.E. 10/12, R. Carr to T. M. Liebenrood, Rotterdam, 25 May 1740, 'We expect our port will be open for the importation of foreign grain, upon this view have already dispatched some ships to Dantzig, but lest our port should be opened some time before they can return, I desire you would advise what you think a cargo of the best E. Country rye might be purchased with you. I don't mean after its being land[ed] with you but to apply to some who have ships on their way from the Baltick, if the price was agreeable [and] the fraught, might send orders to the Sound.'
30. As the following invoice from Carr's correspondence shows (Z.C.E. 10/11, 1738, other particulars lacking):

Charges on barley sold at Amsterdam, 1738

To 40 Last barley	fl. 3360

Charges

Custom at Fl. 3.3 st. p. last	fl. 126.00
Land Duty at 19¾ st. p. last	39.10
Passport Fees	2.16
	168.06
Lighterage, moving &c (more or less)	50
Measuring 8 st. & Breakage 6 st. p. last	28
Commission on fl. 3360 at 2 p. ct	67
	fl. 313.06

31. A striking example of an English exporter completely by-passing the Dutch entrepôt is provided by George Radcliffe of London. After his return from the Levant in 1724, he decided to enter the grain trade and established one of his partners, Henry Croston, at Mahon on the island of Minorca, which was to serve as a granary from which English grain was to be shipped to Mediterranean markets. Croston received information as to the state of the grain market in France, Spain, and Portugal, which was then transmitted to Radcliffe in London. In February 1726 for example, Croston reported, 'Hitherto, the prices on the coast of Spain have been low, but now the time draws on they may be expected to rise; but by all accounts I have, Lisbon is the most promising market which probably the demand in France may still effect. You know best whether it will answer

going farther, though we have it that corn bears a great price in the West parts of France.' Croston in turn received very exact information on the state of the Spanish market from an English house in Alicante, Merrett Hall & Comp., which itself dealt in English grain. (Guildhall Library: Ms 6645/1, Radcliffe Papers, H. Croston to E. Radcliffe & C. Barnardiston, 11 Feb. 1726).

32. GAR: N. Arch. 2332/70 T. M. Liebenrood & J. Moore, 24 Mar. 1738; 2335/420 T. M. Liebenrood & S. Prockter, 22 Apr. 1741.

33. Ibid., 2345/350 W. van Rykevorsel and Son & R. Jeddere, 25 Aug. 1750; 2337/636 D. van der Leven & R. Lindsay, 16 Nov. 1743; 2328/567 Wm. Konink & J. Roxby, 21 Aug. 1734; 1509/509 Declaration of J. & P. Charron, 18 Dec. 1719; 1509/356 A. Hope & F. Seaman, 5 Nov. 1719; 2344/393 I. and Z. Hope & J. Melbourne, 4 Nov. 1749.

34. M. G. Buist, *At Spes Non Fracta: Hope & Co. 1770–1815* (The Hague, 1974) p. 5.

35. Barnes, *English Corn Laws*, p. 15; W. T. Comber, *Inquiry*, pp. 144–5.

36. HUL: Ms D.P./82, Maister Ledger, Mar. 1715 entry:
Hugh Mason Dr. to sundry accounts for Bounty Money on corn.

Nov. 12	John Burridge for 400 qrs wheat p. Rd. Hunter £100				
Dec. 17	do.	900	do.	Miles Walker	225
Jan. 29	do.	600	do.	Ed. Bower	150
do.	do.	500	do.	J. Smales	125
					£600

IV Agrarian Improvement and English Competitiveness

1. Davenant, 'Second Report', p. 408.

2. J. A. Faber, 'Het probleem van de dalende graanaanvoer uit de Oostzeelanden in de tweede helft van de zeventiende eeuw', *Afdeling Agrarische Geschiedenis Bijdragen* 9 (1963), and translated as 'The Decline of the Baltic Grain Trade' in *Acta Historiae Neerlandica* I (1966), to which future references relate.

3. M. Morineau, 'La balance du commerce franco-néerlandais et le resserrement économique des Provinces-Unies au XVIIIème siècle', *Economisch Historisch Jaarboek* XXX (1965) p. 197.

4. John, 'English Agricultural Improvement', pp. 56–7.

5. J. G. van Dillen, 'Stukken betreffende den Amsterdamschen graanhandel omstreeks het jaar 1681', *Economisch Historisch Jaarboek* III (1917) p. 80. Prof. John was mistaken in supposing that malt 'did not figure amongst the Baltic exports' (John, op. cit., p. 57); the parliamentary paper to which he referred excludes grain other than wheat and rye.

6. See above, pp. 30–33.

7. It is in any case possible to date the beginnings of that decline to the 1650s, or possibly even earlier; see M. Bogucka, 'Amsterdam and the Baltic in the First Half of the Seventeenth Century', *Econ. Hist. Rev.*, 2nd ser. XXVI (1973) p. 447, where it is concluded that 'although the Baltic area still constituted Amsterdam's principal grain-base, the first symptoms of the approaching decline of what, in the sixteenth century, the Dutch had called their 'mother trade', were already evident in the first half of the seventeenth century.'

8. Faber, 'Baltic Grain Trade', pp. 123–6.

9. M. Morineau, 'La balance du commerce franco-néerlandais', p. 197; K. Glamann,

'European Trade, 1500–1750', in C. M. Cipolla, *The Fontana Economic History of Europe* 2 (1974 ed.) pp. 464–5; J. de Vries, *The Dutch Rural Economy in the Golden Age, 1500–1700* (New Haven, 1974) p. 171.

10. de Vries, *Dutch Rural Economy*, p. 172.
11. A. Wyczánski, 'Le Niveau de la Récolte des Céréales en Pologne du XVIe au XVIIIe Siècle', *Contributions and Communications, First International Economic History Conference, Stockholm* (Paris, 1960) pp. 585–90.
12. J. Gierowski and A. Kamiński in J. S. Bromley (ed.), *New Cambridge Modern History*, vol. VI (Cambridge, 1970) pp. 704–5.
13. Davenant, 'Second Report', p. 424.
14. C. H. Wilson and G. Parker, *Introduction to the Sources of European Economic History, 1500–1800* (1977) p. 37.
15. H. E. S. Fisher, *Portugal Trade*, p. 29.
16. K. F. Helleiner, 'The Population of Europe' in E. E. Rich and C. H. Wilson (eds.), *The Cambridge Economic History of Europe* IV (Cambridge, 1967) pp. 63–7.
17. It has been estimated that Holland's population declined from 883,000 in 1680 to 783,000 in 1750; for the whole of the United Provinces, population levels were fairly stagnant, at 1.85 to 1.95 millions in 1700, and 1.90 to 1.95 millions in 1750 (J. A. Faber, H. K. Roessingh, B. H. Slicher van Bath, A. M. van der Woude, and H. J. van Xanten, 'Population Changes and Economic Developments in the Netherlands: a historical survey', *AAG Bijdragen* 12 (1965) pp. 60, 110).
18. Consular Reports, Rotterdam, 1765.
19. A. M. van der Woude, 'Het Noorderkwartier. Een regional historisch onderzoek in de demografisch en economische geschiedenis van westelijk Nederland van de late middeleeuwen tot het begin van de negentiende eeuw', *AAG Bijdragen* 16 (1972) II, pp. 585–6, 593–6; III, pp. 840–1.
20. PRO: S. P. 84/429, R. Wolters to Wm. Chetwynd, 30 May 1747; see also S. P. 84/430, ibid., 1 and 22 Sept. 1747; Morineau, 'La balance du commerce franco-néerlandais', pp. 196–8.
21. John, 'English Agricultural Improvement' p. 63.
22. W. Abel, *Agrarkrisen und Agrarkonjunktur im Mitteleuropa vom 13. bis zum 19. Jahrhundert* (Berlin, 1966) pp. 152–3.
23. F. P. Braudel and F. Spooner, 'Prices in Europe from 1450' in E. E. Rich and C. H. Wilson (eds.), *The Cambridge Economic History of Europe* IV, pp. 470–1.
24. NRO: Z.C.E. 10/11, R. Carr to R. Hayes, Konigsberg, 2 Nov. 1738.
25. Ibid., R. Carr to Wm. Norton, Dunkirk, 24 Nov. 1738.
26. Maister Letters, N. Maister to H. Maister, London, 4 Feb. 1738; H. Maister to N. Maister, Hull, 28 Feb. 1738.
27. Comparison of the data contained in Table 7 (pp. 72–3) confirms that transfer costs were wholly absorbed by the bounty, since prices of English grain sold on the Amsterdam Bourse were rarely higher than London prices.
28. A. Smith, *Wealth of Nations*, pp. 223–42; A. Marshall, *Industry and Trade* (1919) pp. 749–50; C. R. Fay, *The Corn Laws and Social England* (Cambridge, 1932) pp. 12–27; T. S. Ashton, *Economic History of England*, pp. 48–50; G. E. Mingay, 'The Agricultural Depression, 1730–1750', *Econ. Hist. Rev.*, 2nd ser. VIII (1956), repr. in Carus-Wilson (ed.), *Essays*, vol. II, p. 323.
29. B. H. Slicher van Bath, *The Agrarian History of Western Europe, 500–1850* (1963) pp. 109–11, 206–20; Braudel and Spooner, 'Prices in Europe from 1450', pp. 470–1.
30. Barnes, *English Corn Laws*, p. 11.
31. N. S. B. Gras, *The Evolution of the English Corn Market* (Cambridge, 1915) pp. 113–14.

32. Calendar of State Papers Domestic, Charles II, T. Holden to J. Williamson, 15 Nov. 1675.
33. Ibid., 6 Dec. 1675.
34. Ibid., T. Aslaby to J. Williamson, 2 Nov. 1675; see also ibid., T. Aslaby to J. Williamson, 20 July 1676, 'Corn is very good and plentiful in these parts [Bridlington], as has been these many years, though the old corn is much drained out of the country by the great quantities daily exported'; also 13 Nov. 1676 and 22 Feb. 1677. Similar reports were received from Deal (21 Nov. 1676) and Stockton (6 Oct. 1676).
35. On the basis of estimates of corn output given in P. Deane and W. A. Cole, *British Economic Growth, 1688–1959* (Cambridge, 1962) Table 17, p. 65.
36. E. L. Jones, 'The Condition of English Agriculture, 1500–1640', *Econ. Hist. Rev.*, 2nd ser. XXI (1968) p. 619; J. Thirsk, 'Seventeenth-Century Agriculture and Social Change', in J. Thirsk (ed.), *Land, Church, and People: essays presented to Prof. H. P. R. Finberg, Agricultural History Review Supplement* (1970) pp. 152, 170; E. Kerridge, *The Agricultural Revolution* (1967) pp. 326–8; B. A. Holderness, *Pre-Industrial England: economy and society from 1500 to 1750* (1976) pp. 62–75.
37. M. Overton, 'Agricultural Change in Norfolk and Suffolk, 1580–1740', (University of Cambridge Ph. D. thesis, 1981); I am grateful to Dr Overton for supplying a copy of the graph on which this statement is based, 'Root crop innovation, sheep and barley valuations, and barley yields, 1585–1735'.
38. M. Overton, 'An Agricultural Revolution, 1650–1750?', *Agricultural History, Papers presented to the Economic History Society Conference* (Canterbury, 1983) p. 12.
39. M. Turner, 'Agricultural Productivity in England in the Eighteenth Century: evidence from crop yields', *Econ. Hist. Rev.,* 2nd ser. XXXV (1982) p. 504.
40. Ibid., p. 490.
41. M. Overton, 'Estimating Crop Yields from Probate Inventories: an example from East Anglia, 1585–1735', *Journal of Economic History*, XXXIX (1979) p. 375.
42. Ibid., pp. 371–2, 375.
43. E. A. Wrigley and R. S. Schofield, *The Population History of England, 1541–1871: a reconstruction* (1981) Appendix 5, p. 577: population totals, estimates (millions).

	Rickman	back projection
1701	5.112	5.058
1711	4.893	5.230
1721	5.197	5.350
1731	5.412	5.263
1741	5.663	5.576
1751	6.039	5.772
1761	6.290	6.147

44. J. D. Chambers, *Population, Economy, and Society in Pre-Industrial England* ed. W. A. Armstrong (1972) p. 23. See also H. J. Habakkuk, *Population Growth and Economic Development since 1750* (Leicester, 1971) pp. 46–8.
45. Chambers, *Population, Economy, and Society*, p. 145.
46. Wrigley and Schofield, *Population History of England*, pp. 78–9: corrected decadal totals of baptisms and burials taken from London bills of mortality.

	baptisms ('000)	burials ('000)
1690–99	164.6	215.5
1700–09	164.5	205.3
1710–19	183.9	227.4

	baptisms ('000)	burials ('000)
1720–29	205.0	263.3
1730–39	197.0	257.9
1740–49	172.9	271.6
1750–59	174.7	225.7

For a detailed contemporary account of the decline in London's population during the second quarter of the eighteenth century, see C. Morris, *Observations on the Past Growth and Present State of the City of London: reprinted from the edition printed at London in 1751; with a continuation of the tables to the end of the year 1757* (1759) pp. 110–17.

47. Chambers, *Population, Economy, and Society*, p. 115.
48. N. S. B. Gras, *English Corn Market*, pp. 183–209; F. J. Fisher, 'The Development of the London Food Market, 1540–1640', *Econ. Hist. Rev.* VII (1937) and repr. in Carus-Wilson, *Essays*, I (1954) pp. 146–51. See also R. B. Westerfield, *Middlemen in English Business, particularly between 1660 and 1760* (New Haven, 1915) p. 133.
49. See above, pp. 37–40.
50. On eighteenth century climate, see D. J. Schove, 'The Preliminary Reduction of Wind and Pressure Observations in N. W. Europe, A.D. 1648–1955', (University of London Ph.D. thesis, 1958) especially p. 127: 'The dryness of the whole period from 1730 to 1766 can be confirmed by rain-gauge records, and the period includes a succession of four dry years (1730–33), three wet years (1734–36) and a fourteen year period (1737–50) in which the mean rainfall must have been at least 10 per cent below the normal'; and pp. 131–2, 'The 1740s have already been compared with the 1940s. The forties of both centuries saw a return of anticyclonic conditions – hot, dry summers and cold, dry winters and springs with very high pressure and frequent north-easterly seasons ... . The rainfall of the decade 1741–50 in N.W. Europe was only 94 per cent of the 1731–60 normal, and that thirty-year period was itself a very dry one ... . Dryness in England, according to an old saying, never caused scarcity, and the decade was indeed one of abundance throughout the British Isles.'
51. J. D. Chambers, 'The Vale of Trent, 1670–1800: a regional study of economic change', *Econ. Hist. Rev. Supplement* 3 (1957) p. 44.
52. Cited by E. L. Jones, *Seasons and Prices: the role of the weather in English agricultural history* (1964) p. 137.
53. Charles Smith, *Three Tracts on the Corn Trade* (1766; 1804 ed.) p. 42.
54. A. Smith, *Wealth of Nations*, p. 91; G. E. Mingay, 'The Agricultural Depression', pp. 321–2.
55. Mingay, 'The Agricultural Depression', p. 324.
56. J. Steuart, *An Inquiry into the Principles of Political Oeconomy* (1767; ed. A. S. Skinner, 1966) I, p. 111.
57. J. Tucker, *A Brief Essay on the Advantages and Disadvantages which respectively attend France and Great Britain with regard to Trade* (1750), referred to by Steuart in the (French) adaptation of this work by Sir John Nickolls.
58. Steuart, *Inquiry*, p. 111.
59. NRO: Z.C.E. 10/11, R. Carr to Wm. Norton, Dunkirk, 24 Nov. 1738.
60. W. Stout, *The Autobiography of William Stout of Lancaster, 1665–1752* ed. J. D. Marshall (Manchester Univ. Press, 1967) p. 213.
61. NRO: Z.C.E. 10/12 R. Carr to T. M. Liebenrood, Rotterdam, 29 Sept. 1739. See also William Stout's comments on the relationship between expectations of price changes and stocks of imported grain, W. Stout, *Autobiography*, p. 206 (1730): 'They continued the importation of corn at Liverpool too long, and there was in Liverpool, in the harvest, thirty three thousand windles of foreign corn, wheat, rye, and barley, and no sale for it

after [the] new came off the ground. Which filled their ware houses so as they had no room for their other merchandize, and it was supposed they lost more by that on hand than they got in the dearth of it.' (The windle amounted to about three bushels).

62. Farmers in the pastoral regions were less hard-pressed during the depressed 1730s and 1740s, see J. V. Beckett, 'Regional Variation and the Agricultural Depression, 1730–50', *Econ. Hist. Rev.*, 2nd ser. XXXV (1982), which relies mainly on Cumbrian evidence.

63. *Gentleman's Magazine* XXII (1752) p. 358.

64. Quoted in T. H. Baker, *Records of the Seasons, Prices of Agricultural Produce and Phenomena observed in the British Isles* [1883] p. 187.

65. E. P. Thompson, 'The Moral Economy of the English Crowd in the Eighteenth Century', *Past & Present* 50 (1971) pp. 77–9.

66. Ashton, *Economic History of England*, pp. 49–50; A. Smith, *Wealth of Nations*, p. 225.

67. C. J. Palmer, *The Perlustration of Great Yarmouth* (Great Yarmouth, 1872–5) I, p. 31.

68. Defoe, *Plan of the English Commerce*, p. 232.

69. John, 'English Agricultural Improvement', p. 61; 'Aspects of English Economic Growth in the First Half of the Eighteenth Century', *Economica* 28 (1961), and reprinted in Carus-Wilson, *Essays* II, p. 364; W. E. Minchinton (ed.), *The Growth of English Overseas Trade in the Seventeenth and Eighteenth Centuries* (1969) p. 43.

70. Keith, 'A General View of the Corn Trade', pp. 278–81.

71. Barnes, *English Corn Laws*, pp. 23–45.

72. See for example, the *Gentleman's Magazine* XXII (1752) pp. 453–5, 561.

73. For the increased concentration on barley production in East Anglia, see M. Overton, 'An Agricultural Revolution, 1650–1750?', pp. 9–10.

V Grain Exports and the Dutch Economy

1. John, 'English Agricultural Improvement', p. 57.

2. See above, pp. 45–7.

3. J. Knoppers, 'Dutch-Baltic Shipping from the Late Seventeenth to the Early Nineteenth Century', (Papers presented to the Fifth Conference on Baltic Studies, Columbia University, May 1976) pp. 8–9.

4. W. Stout, *Autobiography*, pp. 217–18.

5. Joh. de Vries, *De Economische Achteruitgang der Republiek in de Achttiende Eeuw* (Amsterdam, 1959) p. 107.

6. Jan de Vries, *The Dutch Rural Economy in the Golden Age, 1500–1700* (New Haven, 1974) pp. 172–3.

7. Ibid., pp. 236–43.

8. NRO: Z.B.L. 192 (Blackett/Matfer Mss, Blackett Letter Book), John Blackett to Ralph Hall, 12 Mar. 1709.

9. J. A. Faber, *Dure tijden en hongersnoden in preïndustriëel Nederland* (Amsterdam, 1959), p. 9.

10. Ibid., p. 10.

11. See J. Meuvret, 'Les Oscillations des Prix des Céréales aux XVIIe et XVIIIe Siècles en Angleterre et dans les Pays du Bassin Parisien', *Revue d'Histoire Moderne et Contemporaine* 16 (1969) and repr. in Meuvret (ed.), *Études d'Histoire Économique* (Cahiers des Annales, 32, 1971) p. 123.

12. Such as 1698; see J. G. van Dillen, 'Dreigende hongersnood in de Republiek in de laatste jaren der zeventiende eeuw', in J. G. van Dillen, *Mensen en achtergronden; studies, uitgegeven ter gelegenheid van de tachtigste verjaardag van de schrijver* (Groningen, 1964) pp. 193–226; Idem, 'Amsterdam's Role in Seventeenth-Century Dutch Politics and its Economic Background', in J. S. Bromley and E. H. Kossmann, *Britain and the Netherlands in Europe and Asia* II (Groningen, 1964) pp. 145–6.

13. J. Arbuthnot, 'A Short Account of the Corn Trade of Amsterdam' (1773), *Annals of Agriculture* XXVII (1796) p. 370.

14. W. D. Voorthuijsen, *De Republiek der Verenigde Nederlanden en het Mercantilisme* ('S-Gravenhage, 1965) pp. 65–7.

15. J. Hovy, *Het voorstel van 1751 tot instelling van een beperkt vrijhavenstelsel in de Republiek* (Groningen, 1966) pp. 483–5.

16. Ibid., p. 131.

17. See the 'Commentary' by Jan de Vries in Krantz and Hohenberg, *Failed Transitions*, p. 55.

18. Hovy, *Het voorstel van 1751*, p. 484 n. 234.

19. Ibid., p. 483–4.

20. PRO: C.O.389/18, Davenant's 'Memorial to the Lord Treasurer concerning the free trade now carried on between France and Holland', 17 Dec. 1705.

21. See above, p. 43.

22. PRO: S.P.84/517, R. Wolters to Wm. Frazer, 12 Dec. 1767, 'All most all the wheat that comes to this market [Rotterdam] is bought up, to be sent to some part of England.'

23. Davenant, 'Second Report', p. 425; see also Westerfield, *Middlemen in English Business*, p. 163.

24. J. G. van Dillen, 'Economic Fluctuations and Trade in the Netherlands, 1650–1750', in P. Earle (ed.), *Essays in European Economic History, 1500–1800* (Oxford, 1974) p. 202; Knoppers, 'Dutch-Baltic Shipping', p. 9.

25. PRO: S.P.84/527, R. Wolters to R. Sutton, 7 Sept. 1770.

26. W. S. Unger, 'Trade through the Sound in the Seventeenth and Eighteenth Centuries', *Econ. Hist. Rev.*, 2nd ser. XII (1960) pp. 213–14.

27. van Dillen, 'Economic Fluctuations', p. 203; van Dillen added that these changes in Dutch-Baltic trade did not completely compensate for the decline of the grain trade.

28. Unger, 'Trade through the Sound', pp. 212, 215.

29. Knoppers, 'Dutch-Baltic Shipping', p. 6. It must be emphasised, however, that the Dutch share of the Baltic trade declined.

30. J. G. van Dillen, *Van Rijkdom en Regenten: Handboek tot de economische en sociale geschiedenis van Nederland tijdens de Republiek* ('s-Gravenhage, 1970) p. 560.

31. Ibid., p. 562.

32. Faber, *Dure tijden*, pp. 7–8.

33. S. Schama, *Patriots and Liberators: revolution in the Netherlands, 1780–1813* (1977) p. 29.

34. P. Jansen, 'Armoede in Amsterdam aan het eind van de achttiende eeuw', *Tijdschrift voor Geschiedenis* 88 (1975) pp. 613–25.

35. P. Jansen, 'Het ritme van de dood: sociale conjunctuur in Amsterdam, 1750–1800', *Ons Amsterdam* (Mar. 1973) pp. 24–7.

36. Ibid., pp. 26–7. The first economic crisis in the Netherlands which did not coincide with high grain prices was that of 1857.

37. See above, pp. 28–31.

38. C. Visser, *Verkeersindustrieen te Rotterdam in de tweede helft der achttiende eeuw* (Rotterdam, 1927) pp. 93–7.
39. J. A. van Houtte, *An Economic History of the Low Countries, 800–1800* (1977) pp. 255–6.
40. Joh. de Vries, *Economische Achteruitgang*, pp. 91–2.
41. Ibid.
42. Visser, *Verkeersindustrieen te Rotterdam*, pp. 59–61.
43. Hovy, *Het voorstel van 1751*, pp. 484 n. 235, 485.
44. Consular Reports, Rotterdam, 1765.

VI Grain Exports and the English Economy

1. G. N. Clark, *Guide to English Commercial Statistics, 1696–1782* (1938) pp. 10–12.
2. Customs 48/11, 9 Nov. 1717. For East Anglian barley prices, see R. A. C. Parker, *Coke of Norfolk: a financial and agricultural study, 1707–1842* (Oxford, 1975) p. 209.
3. E. B. Schumpeter, *English Overseas Trade Statistics, 1697–1808* with an Introduction by T. S. Ashton (Oxford, 1960) Table III, p. 16; R. Davis, 'English Foreign Trade, 1700–1774', *Econ. Hist. Rev.*, 2nd ser. XV (1962) *passim*. See also G. N. Clark, *Guide*, p. 34.
4. Professor John described the shortages of these years as 'exceptional occurrences' and suggested that 'much more common were years of large surpluses. In 1713, for instance, cereals amounted to 13 per cent of domestic exports in terms of official values, 18.5 per cent in 1734, 15.8 per cent in 1738 and in the peak year 1750, almost 20 per cent.' This is to substitute one set of exceptional years for another: 1713 was the peak year for wheat exports in that decade; 1734 and 1738 were similar peaks in the 1730s; and 1750 was the peak year of the century.
5. This is demonstrated by the data in Table 7.
6. R. Davis, *The Rise of the English Shipping Industry in the Seventeenth and Eighteenth Centuries* (1962) p. 185. It should be noted however that these estimates exaggerate the tonnage of shipping required in the case of both grain and coal exports, see below, note 12.
7. Defoe, *Plan of the English Commerce*, p. 231.
8. Davis, *Rise of the English Shipping Industry*, p. 185: during the years 1699–1701, an average of 74 per cent of English grain cargoes were destined for nearby Europe, while in 1752–4, the figure was 69 per cent; PRO: C.O. 388/18 Part I, f.22 (1710–14).
9. Maister Letters, N. Maister to H. Maister, London, 6 Mar. 1738.
10. Knoppers, 'Dutch-Baltic Shipping', Table 1, p. 29. This figure relates to Dutch shipping from the Baltic to Amsterdam from 1709 to 1750; tonnages ranged from 140.9 to 206.3 tons.
11. Customs 97/11, 18 Nov. 1738.
12. Leaving aside the question of false entries, the extraction of coal export figures from the Inspector General's ledgers poses considerable problems, since there were innumerable local variations in the size of the chaldron, in which coal exports were measured. 'The same measure did not always mean the same thing in different districts, or even in the same district at different periods,' (J. U. Nef, *The Rise of the British Coal Industry* (1932) II, Appendix C on weights and measures, pp. 367–71; see also Customs 85/4 (Sunderland) 20 Feb. 1755 on variations in the size of the Winchester chaldron in the eighteenth century). The problem is not of course peculiar to the coal trade – it also existed in a minor

form in the grain trade where the quarter was likewise not a uniform measure – but because of the low value/bulk ratio and the heavy burden of taxes on coal which tended to increase the content of a given measure over time, the problem is especially serious in this particular trade which required more shipping tonnage than any other.

The most substantial errors arise from the fact that coal exports to nearby Europe, originating mainly from the north-east, were measured in Newcastle and Sunderland chaldrons equivalent to about 53 cwt, while exports to Ireland, shipped mainly from Whitehaven, were measured in Winchester chaldrons of about 27 cwt; see L. M. Cullen, *Anglo-Irish Trade, 1660–1800* (Manchester, 1968) p. 79, where comparison is made between English and Irish customs statistics. The Inspectors General made the formal assumption that all returns were made in London chaldrons, without attempting to make the necessary adjustment; Prof. Davis assumed that the Ledgers recorded Newcastle chaldrons (*Rise of the English Shipping Industry*, p. 185); while Mrs Schumpeter seems to have assumed London (Winton) measure, (op. cit., Tables VII & VIII, pp. 19–24). Through his work on Port Books *and* Customs Ledgers, Nef became aware of internal inconsistencies in the recording of coal exports, but did not identify their source (op. cit., II, p. 385 n.1.).

Among other things, this error has resulted in an exaggerated view of the importance of the Irish coal trade in relation to other overseas markets (e.g. T. S. Ashton and J. Sykes, *The Coal Industry of the Eighteenth Century* (Manchester, 1929) p. 227), and has produced over-generous estimates of the amount of shipping employed in the coal export trade. The estimates given in Table 9 therefore incorporate corrected figures for Irish coal exports; and an adjustment has been made to take account of specific known abuses involving under-declaration of exports at Sunderland from 1717 to 1747 (see Ormrod, 'Anglo-Dutch Commerce', pp. 266–70). Nevertheless, the fact remains that these figures represent an underestimate because of the widespread extent of under-declaration of coal exports.

13. B. R. Mitchell and P. Deane, *Abstract of British Historical Statistics* (Cambridge, 1962) pp. 112–13.
14. Consular Reports, Rotterdam, 1765.
15. Davis, *Rise of the English Shipping Industry*, pp. 191–2.
16. NRO: Z.C.E. 10/16, R. Carr to D. van Dam, Rotterdam, 10 June 1745.
17. The malt trade was fairly regular throughout the year; see Customs 97/8, 4 Jan. 1734, showing the seasonal pattern of grain exports from Yarmouth, 1733 ('000 quarters):

	Wheat	Rye	Barley	Malt
Lady Day quarter	11.1	2.1	7.0	27.1
Midsummer do.	5.4	1.1	2.2	22.1
Michaelmas do.	4.8	1.1	–	22.0
Christmas do.	7.3	1.6	0.1	27.8

18. E. Hughes, *North Country Life in the Eighteenth Century: the North East, 1700–1750* (1952) pp. 55–6; GAR: N. Arch. 2328/108, 116, 167, 239, 484, 567, 599.
19. Davis, *Rise of the English Shipping Industry*, p. 194: 'Because there was, for one reason or another, much under-utilisation of capacity, there were important reserves available to deal with specially large crops, whether of sugar or tobacco across the ocean, or of corn in East Anglia.'
20. GAR: N. Arch. 2328/804, 10 Nov. 1734, and 2328/108 & 116,24 Feb. 1734. Other examples include the *Mary* of Dartmouth, 2325/197,3 Aug. 1731 (coal, Milford Haven-R'dam) & 2325/286, 20 Nov. 1731 (grain, R'dam-Poole & London); the *Batchelour* of Plymouth, 2332/70, 24 Mar. 1738 (grain to Lisbon & Cadiz) & 2328/80, 16 Feb. 1734

(coal, Sunderland-Christiansand; timber, Christiansand-R'dam); the *Providence* of
Sunderland, 2116/418, 28 Mar. 1732 (coal, Newcastle-R'dam) & 2335/420,22 Apr. 1741
(grain, R'dam-Newcastle).

21. GAR: N. Arch. 2335/281, 31 Mar. 1741; 2335/559, 1 June 1741; 2335/738, 20 July 1741;
2335/487, 12 May 1741; 2108/469, 30 Apr. 1728.

22. GAR: N. Arch. 2335/265, 26 Oct. 1731 (the *Virtue* of Yarmouth, Yarmouth-Newcastle-
Gibraltar with coal); 2328/674, 1 Oct 1734 (the *Endeavour* of Blakeney, Newcastle-
Christiansand with coal).

23. NRO: Z.C.E.10/11 R. Carr to Wm. Norton, Dunkirk, 27 Dec. 1738.

24. GAA: Brants 1337, J. Coutts & Co. to J. I. de Neufville, Amsterdam, 13 Feb. 1748. See
also loc. cit., 19 Aug. 1749 when it was complained that the demands of the fishing trade
were aggravating the scarcity of outward shipping. At this time, Coutts & Co. were making
regular use of Dutch ships and masters.

25. Maister Letters, N. Maister to H. Maister, London 5 and 29 Apr. 1738.

26. See Ormrod, 'Anglo-Dutch Commerce', pp. 351–60.

27. NRO: Z.C.E.10/12, R. Carr to Wm. Norton, Dunkirk, 24 Apr. 1740.

28. Ormrod, 'Anglo-Dutch Commerce', Table 26, p. 358.

29. Consular Reports, Rotterdam, 1765.

30. PRO: S.P. 84/430, R. Wolters to Wm. Chetwynd, London, 8 Dec. 1747; loc. cit., 22
Sept. 1747.

31. Ormrod, 'Anglo-Dutch Commerce', pp. 360–7.

32. Customs 97/3, 25 Mar. 1715.

33. Ormrod, 'Anglo-Dutch Commerce', pp. 284–320.

34. *The Case of British Merchants, Owners of Ships, relative to the Employment and Increase of British
Shipping, and British Navigators* (1750) p. 1, no. 6437 in L. W. Hanson, *Contemporary Printed
Sources for British and Irish Economic History, 1701–1750* (Cambridge, 1963). Charter-parties
in the Rotterdam notarial archives show that triangular trade between Holland, England
and Norway was well-established, though most relate to voyages in the direction
Rotterdam-England-Norway.

35. H. S. K. Kent, *War and Trade in Northern Seas: Anglo-Scandinavian economic relations in the mid-
eighteenth century* (Cambridge, 1973) pp. 94–5.

36. Guildhall Library: Ms 6645/1, H. Croston to G. Radcliffe, London, 23 Dec. 1725.

37. Barnes, *English Corn Laws*, p. 11. Although Adam Smith argued that it served mainly
commercial interests; Fay, *The Corn Laws*, p. 15.

38. See above, p. 16.

39. Arthur Young's arguments may be taken as being typical of those defending the bounty
policy, e.g. *The Expediency of a Free Exportation of Corn at this Time* (1770), summarised by
Barnes, *English Corn Laws*, pp. 27–8. Adam Smith's arguments against the bounty policy
were summarised by Lipson, *The Economic History of England* (1931) II, pp. 451–64.

40. Fay, *The Corn Laws*, p. 22.

41. George Chalmers described Combrune as 'a brewer at Hampstead, and who leaving off
that business settled in Mary[le]bone. He was supposed to understand the corn trade
well. And was employed about the year 1773 to make some calculations on that trade for
[the] government. He wrote an esteemed tract on brewing' (Ms note by Chalmers in his
copy of Combrune, *Enquiry*, deposited in the Goldsmiths' Library, London).

42. C. Smith, *Tracts on the Corn Trade*, pp. 115–16.

43. A. Young, *The Farmer's Letters to the People of England* (2nd ed. 1768) pp. 18–19.

44. Combrune, *Enquiry*, pp. 108–10.

45. W. Temple, loc. cit.

46. BL: Add. Ms. 8133B f.99, 'Observations on the Laws for regulating the Importation and

Exportation of Corn', June 1783, by Wm. Arnold, Collector of Customs at Cowes.

47. Barnes, *English Corn Laws*, pp. 18–19.
48. Expressed as a percentage deviation from a nine-year moving average. Sources:

Amsterdam	BPP XVI (1826–7), Consuls' Reports.
London	Combrune, *Enquiry*, p. 74.
Ancona and Corunna	J. Marshall, *A Digest for all the Accounts* (1833) p. 98.
Leipzig	M. J. Elsas, *Umriss einer Geschichte der Preise und Lohne in Deutschland* (Leiden, 1940) pp. 519–20.
Douai	A. P. Usher, 'The General Course of Wheat Prices in France, 1350–1788', *Review of Economic Statistics* XII (1930) p. 161.

For a comparison of fluctuations in English and French cereal prices, which emphasises the instability of French grain supplies, but perhaps overstates the moderating influence of the Corn Laws on English prices, see J. Meuvret, 'Les Oscillations des Prix des Céréales', pp. 113–24.

For a contemporary comparison of Spanish and English grain supply, see G. de Uztariz, *The Theory and Practice of Commerce and Maritime Affairs* (trans. J. Kippax, 1751) vol. II, p. 195.

49. C. W. J. Granger and C. M. Elliott, 'A Fresh Look at Wheat Prices and Markets in the Eighteenth Century', *Econ. Hist. Rev.*, 2nd ser. XX (1967) p. 262.
50. Combrune, *Enquiry*, pp. 95–6.
51. PRO: C.O. 388/12, 'An Account of the Market Prices of Corn & Grain according to the Returns made to the Commrs. General Enquiry of the 17 March 1709'. Returns were received from 32 English ports; because inland markets are excluded, it is to be expected that this data will understate the true extent of price differences over the country as a whole. Figure 6 expresses the price at each port as a percentage deviation from the average.
52. This is suggested by the returns themselves which contain complete quotations of rye prices for these two regions, the general level of which is lower than the occasional quotations of rye prices at ports outside these regions.
53. C. Smith, *Tracts on the Corn Trade*, p. 33.
54. Barnes, *English Corn Laws*, p. 13.
55. 11 Geo. II, c. 22. See Appendix 3 (iii) pp. 104–7.
56. D. G. D. Isaac, 'A Study of Popular Disturbances in Britain, 1714–1754', (University of Edinburgh Ph.D. thesis, 1953) pp. 48–9.
57. See however, E. P. Thompson, 'The Moral Economy', pp. 76–136; R. B. Rose, 'Eighteenth Century Price Riots and Public Policy in England', *International Review of Social History* VI (1961) pp. 277–92; Isaac, 'Popular Disturbances in Britain', pp. 1–50. The fullest account yet available is that provided by the contributors to A. Charlesworth (ed.), *An Atlas of Rural Protest in Britain, 1548–1900* (1982), which indicates the geographical distribution of food riots, distinguishing the different forms of action taken, and from which the above figures are derived, pp. 80–92.
58. Isaac, 'Popular Disturbances in Britain', pp. 2–7.
59. Rose, 'Eighteenth Century Price Riots', p. 289.
60. Rose distinguishes four distinct categories: spontaneous looting; riots directed against the transportation and export of corn; direct action by rioters to impose fixed prices on the market; and attempts to force local magistrates to decree maximum prices by mob pressure (ibid., p. 279).
61. Ibid., p. 281.
62. Ashton, *Economic History of England*, p. 4.

63. Chambers, *The Vale of Trent*, p. 29.
64. W. Stout, *Autobiography*, p. 201.
65. Chambers, *Population, Economy and Society*, chapter 4.
66 A. B. Appleby, 'Grain Prices and Subsistence Crises in England and France, 1590–1740', *Journal of Economic History* XXXIX (1979) p. 885.
67. Ibid., p. 882.
68. Wrigley and Schofield, *Population History of England*, pull-out graph 1.
69. Ibid., p. 334, Table 8.12, and p. 310.
70. Chambers, *Population, Economy and Society*, p. 93.
71. Ashton, *Economic History of England*, p. 48.
72. *Gentleman's Magazine* (1752), extract of a letter from the *General Evening Post*, 25 Aug. 1752.
73. House of Lords Record Office, Main Papers HL, 19 Mar. 1765, T. Brock, Town Clerk of Chester to the Earl of Abercorn, 11 Mar. 1765. This is almost identical to Adam Smith's view.
74. Mingay, 'Agricultural Depression', *passim*; J. D. Chambers and G. E. Mingay, *The Agricultural Revolution, 1750–1880* (1966) pp. 40–3; G. E. Mingay, *English Landed Society in the Eighteenth Century* (1963) pp. 54–6.
75. John, 'Aspects of Economic Growth', *passim*; 'Agricultural Productivity and Economic Growth in England, 1700–1760', *Journal of Economic History* XXV (1965) *passim*; 'English Agricultural Improvement', pp. 62–3. The literature challenging these views is summarised by A. J. Little, *Deceleration in the Eighteenth-Century British Economy* (1976).
76. E. L. Jones, 'English and European Agricultural Development, 1650–1750', in R. M. Hartwell (ed.), *The Industrial Revolution* (1970) p. 43.
77. Krantz and Hohenberg, *Failed Transitions*, p. 79.
78. *Gentleman's Magazine* (1752) p. 358.
79. R. Brenner, 'Agrarian Class Structure and Economic Development', p. 64.
80. In the discussions arising from Brenner's 'Agrarian Class Structure and Economic Development' in the journal *Past and Present*, vols. 78, 79, 80 (1978).
81. Jan de Vries, *The Dutch Rural Economy*, p. 237.
82. Marx, *Capital*, vol. III p. 324.

Bibliography

Abel, W.	*Agrarkrisen und Agrarkonjunktur im Mitteleuropa vom 13. bis zum 19. Jahrhundert* (Berlin, 1935; 3rd ed. Berlin 1966; trans. O. Ordish 1980 as *Agricultural Fluctuations in Europe*).
Althusser, L.	*Lenin and Philosophy, and Other Essays* (1971).
Appleby, A. B.	'Grain Prices and Subsistence Crises in England and France, 1590–1740', *Journal of Economic History*, 39 (1979).
Arbuthnot, J.	'A Short Account of the Corn Trade of Amsterdam 1773', *Annals of Agriculture* XXVII (1796).
Aron, P. H.	'M. N. Pokrovskii and the Impact of the First Five-Year Plan on Soviet Historiography', in J. S. Curtiss (ed.) *Essays in Russian and Soviet Historiography* (New York, 1963).
Ashton, T. S. and Sykes, J.	*The Coal Industry of the Eighteenth Century* (Manchester Univ. Press, 1929).
Ashton, T. S.	*An Economic History of England: the 18th century* (1955).
Baker, D.	'The Marketing of Corn in the First Half of the Eighteenth Century: North-East Kent', *Agricultural History Review* 18 (1970).
Baker, T. H.	*Records of the Seasons, Prices of Agricultural Produce and Phenomena observed in the British Isles* [1883].
Barber, J.	'The Establishment of Intellectual Orthodoxy in the U.S.S.R., 1928–1934', *Past and Present* 83 (1979).
Barnes, D. G.	*History of the English Corn Laws from 1660–1846* (1930).
Beckett, J. V.	'Regional Variation and the Agricultural Depression, 1730–50, *Econ. Hist. Rev.*, 2nd ser. XXXV (1973).
Bogucka, M.	'Amsterdam and the Baltic in the First Half of the Seventeenth Century', *Econ. Hist. Rev.*, 2nd ser. XXVI (1973).
Bois, G.	'Against the Neo-Malthusian Orthodoxy', *Past and Present* 79 (1978).
Braudel, F. P. and Spooner, F.	'Prices in Europe from 1450' in E. E. Rich and C. H. Wilson (eds.), *The Cambridge Economic History of Europe*, vol. IV: *The Economy of Expanding Europe in the 16th and 17th Centuries* (Cambridge, 1967).
Brenner, R.	'The Origins of Capitalist Development: a critique of Neo-Smithian Marxism', *New Left Review* 104 (1977).
Brenner, R.	'Agrarian Class Structure and Economic Development in Pre-Industrial Europe', *Past and Present* 70 (1976).
Brenner, R.	'Dobb on the Transition from Feudalism to Capitalism', *Cambridge Journal of Economics* 2 (1978).
Brenner, R.	'The Agrarian Roots of European Capitalism', *Past and Present* 97 (1982).

133

Buist, M. G.	*At Spes Non Fracta: Hope & Co. 1770–1815* (The Hague, 1974).
Burrish, O.	*Batavia Illustrata* (1728).

Carus-Wilson, E. M.	*Essays in Economic History*, vol. I (1954), vol. II (1962).
Chambers, J. D.	*The Vale of Trent, 1670–1800: a regional study of economic change* (Supplement 3 to the *Economic History Review*, 1957).
Chambers, J. D.	*Population, Economy and Society in Pre-Industrial England*, ed. W. A. Armstrong (1972).
Chambers, J. D. and Mingay, G. E.	*The Agricultural Revolution, 1750–1880* (1966).
Charlesworth, A.	*An Atlas of Rural Protest in Britain, 1548–1900* (London and Canberra, 1983).
Clark, G. N.	*Guide to English Commercial Statistics, 1696–1782* (1938).
Coleman, D. C.	'Industrial Growth and Industrial Revolutions', *Economica*, n.s. XXIII (1956).
Comber, W. T.	*An Inquiry into the State of National Subsistence as connected with the Progress of Wealth and Population* (1808).
Combrune, M.	*An Enquiry into the Prices of Wheat, Malt, and Occasionally of Other Provisions* (1768).
Cooper, J. P.	'In Search of Agrarian Capitalism', *Past and Present* 80 (1978).
Croot, P. and Parker, D.	'Agrarian Class Structure and Economic Development in Pre-Industrial Europe', *Past and Present* 78 (1978).
Cullen, L. M.	*Anglo-Irish Trade, 1660–1800* (Manchester Univ. Press, 1968).

Davenant, C.	'A Second Report to the Commissioners for Stating the Public Accounts' (1711), in Sir C. Whitworth (ed.), *The Political and Commercial Works of . . . Charles Davenant*, vol. V (1771).
Davis, R.	'English Foreign Trade, 1700–1774', *Econ. Hist. Rev.*, 2nd ser. XV (1962), repr. in Minchinton, W.E.
Davis, R.	*The Rise of the English Shipping Industry in the Seventeenth and Eighteenth Centuries* (1962).
Deane, P. and Cole, W. A.	*British Economic Growth, 1688–1959* (Cambridge, 1962; repr. 1964).
Defoe, D.	*A Plan of the English Commerce* (1728).
Dillen, J. G. van	'Stukken betreffende den Amsterdamschen graanhandel omstreeks het jaar 1681', *Economisch Historisch Jaarboek* III (1917).
Dillen, J. G. van	'Dreigende hongersnood in de Republiek in de laatste jaren der zeventiende eeuw', in J. G. Van Dillen (ed.), *Mensen en achtergronden: studies uitgegeven ter gelegenheid van de tachtigste verjaardag van de schrijver* (Groningen, 1964).
Dillen, J. G. van	'Amsterdam's Role in Seventeenth-Century Dutch Politics and its Economic Background', in J. S. Bromley and E. H. Kossmann, *Britain and the Netherlands in Europe and Asia*, vol. II (Groningen, 1964).
Dillen, J. G. van	*Van Rijkdom en Regenten: handboek tot de economische en sociale geschiedenis van Nederland tijdens de Republiek* ('S-Gravenhage, 1970).
Dillen, J. G. van	'Economic Fluctuations and Trade in the Netherlands, 1650–1750',

	in P. Earle (ed.) *Essays in European Economic History, 1500–1800* (Oxford, 1974).
Dobb, M.	*Studies in the Development of Capitalism* (1946).
Dobb, M.	'The Transition from Feudalism to Capitalism', *Science and Society* XXVII (1964), and repr. in M. Dobb, *Papers on Capitalism, Development and Planning* (1967).
Dobb, M.	'From Feudalism to Capitalism', *Marxism Today* (Sept. 1962), reprinted in R. Hilton (ed.), *The Transition from Feudalism to Capitalism* (1976).

Faber, J. A.	*Dure tijden en hongersnoden in preindustriëel Nederland* (Amsterdam, 1959).
Faber, J. A.	'Het probleem van de dalende graanaanvoer uit de Oostzeelanden in de tweede helft van de zeventiende eeuw', *AAG Bijdragen* 9 (1963), and translated as 'The Decline of the Baltic Grain Trade in the Second Half of the Seventeenth Century' in *Acta Historiae Neerlandica* 1 (1966).
Faber, J.A., Roessingh, H.K., Slicher van Bath, B.H., van der Woude, A.M., and van Xanten, H.F.	'Population Changes and Economic Developments in the Netherlands: a historical survey', *AAG Bijdragen* 12 (1965).
Fay, C. R.	*The Corn Laws and Social England* (Cambridge, 1932).
Fisher, F. J.	'The Development of the London Food Market, 1540–1640', *Econ. Hist. Rev.* V (1935), repr. in Carus-Wilson, *Essays*, vol. I.
Fisher, H. E. S.	*The Portugal Trade* (1971).
Forbes, W.	*Memoirs of a Banking-House* [1803] (Edinburgh, 1859).

Gierowski J. and Kaminski A.	'The Eclipse of Poland', chapter XX(2) in J. S. Bromley (ed.), *The New Cambridge Modern History*, vol. VI: *the Rise of Great Britain and Russia, 1688–1715/25* (Cambridge, 1970).
Glamann, K.	'European Trade, 1500–1750', in C. M. Cipolla, *The Fontana Economic History of Europe: the sixteenth and seventeenth centuries*, vol. 2 (1974).
Granger, C. W. J. and Elliott, C. M.	'A Fresh Look at Wheat Prices and Markets in the Eighteenth Century', *Econ. Hist. Rev.*, 2nd ser. XX (1967).
Gras, N. S. B.	*The Evolution of the English Corn Market* (Cambridge, 1915).

Habakkuk, H. J.	'La disparition du paysan anglais', *Annales ESC* XX (1965).
Habakkuk, H. J.	*Population Growth and Economic Development since 1750* (Leicester, 1971).
Hazelkorn, E.	'Some Problems with Marx's Theory of Capitalist Penetration into Agriculture: the case of Ireland', *Economy and Society* 10 (1981).
Heckscher, E. F.	*Mercantilism*, 2 vols (1931).
Helleiner, K. F.	'The Population of Europe', in E. E. Rich and C. H. Wilson (eds.), *The Cambridge Economic History of Europe*, vol. IV (Cambridge, 1967).

Hilton, R. H. (ed.)   *The Transition from Feudalism to Capitalism* (1976).

Hindess, B. and   *Pre-Capitalist Modes of Production* (1974).
Hirst, P.

Hobsbawm, E. J.   'Perry Anderson's History', author's transcript of a lecture given at the University of Kent, Canterbury, May 1976; from a sound recording located in the Audio-Visual Aids Library, University of Kent.

Hobsbawm, E. J.   'Capitalisme et Agriculture: les Réformateurs Écossais au XVIIIe Siècle', *Annales ESC* 3 (1978).

Hobsbawm, E. J.   'The Historians' Group of the Communist Party', in M. Cornforth (ed.), *Rebels and their Causes: essays in honour of A. L. Morton* (1978).

Holderness, B. A.   *Pre-Industrial England: economy and society from 1500 to 1750* (1976).

Houtte, J. A. van   *An Economic History of the Low Countries, 800–1800* (1977).

Hovy, J.   *Het voorstel van 1751 tot instelling van een beperkt vrijhavenstelsel in de Republiek* (Groningen, 1966).

Hughes, E.   *North Country Life in the Eighteenth Century: the North East, 1700–1750* (1952).

Isaac, D.G.D.   'A Study of Popular Disturbances in Britain, 1714–1754', (University of Edinburgh Ph.D. thesis, 1953).

Jack. S. M.   *Trade and Industry in Tudor and Stuart England* (1977).

Jackson, G.   *Hull in the Eighteenth Century* (1972).

Jansen, P.   'Het ritme van de dood: sociale conjunctuur in Amsterdam, 1750–1800', *Ons Amsterdam* (March 1973).

Jansen, P.   'Armoede in Amsterdam aan het eind van de achttiende eeuw', *Tijdschrift voor Geschiedenis* 88 (1975).

John, A. H.   'The Course of Agricultural Change, 1660–1760', in L. S. Pressnell (ed.), *Studies in the Industrial Revolution: essays presented to T. S. Ashton* (1960).

John, A. H.   'Aspects of English Economic Growth in the First Half of the Eighteenth Century', *Economica*, n.s. XXVIII (1961), repr. in Carus-Wilson, *Essays*, vol. II.

John, A. H.   'Agricultural Productivity and Economic Growth in England, 1700–1760', *Journal of Economic History* XXV (1965).

John, A. H.   'English Agricultural Improvement and Grain Exports, 1660–1765' in D. C. Coleman and A. H. John (eds.), *Trade, Government and Economy in Pre-Industrial England: essays presented to F. J. Fisher* (1976).

Jones, E. L.   *Seasons and Prices: the role of the weather in English agricultural history* (1964).

Jones, E. L.   'The Agricultural Origins of Industry', *Past and Present* 40 (1968).

Jones, E. L.   'The Condition of English Agriculture, 1500–1640', *Econ. Hist. Rev.*, 2nd ser. XXI (1968).

Jones, E. L.   'English and European Agricultural Development, 1650–1750', in R. M. Hartwell (ed.), *The Industrial Revolution* (1970).

Kautsky, K.   *Die agrarfrage; eine uebersicht über die tendenzen der modernen landwirthschaft und die agrarpolitik der sozialdemokratie* (Stuttgart, 1899).

Bibliography

Keith, G. S.	'A General View of the Corn Trade and Corn Laws of Great Britain', *Farmer's Magazine* XI (1802).
Kent, H. S. K.	*War and Trade in Northern Seas: Anglo-Scandinavian economic relations in the mid-eighteenth century* (Cambridge, 1973).
Kerridge, E.	'The Movement of Rent, 1540–1640', *Econ. Hist. Rev.* 2nd ser., VI (1953), repr. in Carus-Wilson, *Essays*, vol. II.
Kerridge, E.	*The Agricultural Revolution* (1967).
Kerridge, E. (ed.)	*Agrarian Problems in the Sixteenth Century and After* (1969).
Knoppers, J.	'Dutch-Baltic Shipping from the Late Seventeenth to the Early Nineteenth Century' (paper presented to the Fifth Conference on Baltic Studies, Columbia University, May 1976).
Krantz, F. and Hohenberg, P.	*Failed Transitions to Modern Industrial Society: Renaissance Italy and Seventeenth Century Holland* (Montreal, 1974).
Kriedte, P., Medick, H. and Schlumbohm, J.	*Industrialisation Before Industrialisation: rural industry in the genesis of capitalism* (Cambridge, 1981).
Lipson, E.	*The Economic History of England* 3 vols (vol. 1, 1915; vols. 2 and 3, 1931).
Little, A. J.	*Deceleration in the Eighteenth-Century British Economy* (1976).
Marshall, A.	*Industry and Trade* (1919).
Marx, K.	*Grundrisse* (1857/8; Pelican ed., 1973).
Marx, K.	*Theories of Surplus Value* (1862; repr. Lawrence and Wishart, 1951).
Marx, K.	*Capital* 3 vols (vol. I, 1867, Moscow ed., 1954; vol. II, 1885, Moscow ed., 1957; vol. III, 1894, Moscow ed., 1959).
Mathias, P.	*The Brewing Industry in England, 1700–1830* (Cambridge, 1959).
Medick, H.	'The Proto-Industrial Family Economy: the structural function of household and family during the transition from peasant society to industrial capitalism', *Social History* 3 (1976).
Meuvret, J.	'Les Oscillations des Prix des Céréales aux XVIIe et XVIIIe Siècles en Angleterre et dans les Pays du Bassin Parisien', *Revue d'Histoire Moderne et Contemporaine* 16 (1969) and repr. in J. Meuvret (ed.), *Études d'Histoire Économique* (Cahiers des Annales, 32, 1971).
Minchinton, W. E.	*The Growth of English Overseas Trade in the Seventeenth and Eighteenth Centuries* (1969).
Mingay, G. E.	'The Agricultural Depression, 1730–1750', *Econ. Hist. Rev.*, 2nd ser. VIII (1956), repr. in Carus-Wilson, *Essays*, vol. II.
Mingay, G. E.	*English Landed Society in the Eighteenth Century* (1963).
Mingay, G. E.	*Enclosure and the Small Farmer in the Age of the Industrial Revolution* (Economic History Society, 1968).
Morineau, M.	'La balance du commerce franco-néerlandais et le resserrement économique des Provinces-Unies au XVIII ème siècle', *Economisch Historisch Jaarboek* XXX (1965).
Morris, C.	*Observations on the Past Growth and Present State of the City of London: reprinted from the edition printed at London in 1751; with a continuation of the tables to the end of the year 1757* (1759).

Nef, J. U.   *The Rise of the British Coal Industry*, 2 vols (1932).
Nef, J. U.   'The Progress of Technology and the Growth of Large-Scale Indus-
                    try in Great Britain, 1540–1640', *Economic History Review* V (1934–5)
                    repr. in Carus-Wilson, *Essays*, vol. I.

Ormrod, D. J.   'Anglo-Dutch Commerce, 1700–1760' (University of Cambridge
                    Ph.D. thesis, 1973).
Ormrod, D. J.   'Dutch Commercial and Industrial Decline and British Growth in
                    the Late Seventeenth and Early Eighteenth Centuries', in F. Krantz
                    and P. Hohenberg, *Failed Transitions*.
Ormrod, D. J.   'R. H. Tawney and the Origins of Capitalism', *History Workshop Journal*
                    18 (1984).
Outhwaite, R. B.   'Food Crises in Early Modern England: patterns of public response',
                    in *Proceedings of the Seventh International Economic History Congress*, vol.
                    2, ed. M. Flinn (Edinburgh, 1978).
Outhwaite, R. B.   'Dearth and Government Intervention in English Grain Markets,
                    1590–1700', *Econ. Hist. Rev.*, 2nd ser. XXXIV (1981).
Overton, M.   'Estimating Crop Yields from Probate Inventories: an example
                    from East Anglia, 1585–1735', *Journal of Economic History* XXXIX
                    (1979).
Overton, M.   'Agricultural Change in Norfolk and Suffolk, 1580–1740' (Univer-
                    sity of Cambridge Ph.D. thesis, 1981).
Overton, M.   'An Agricultural Revolution, 1650–1750?', *Agricultural History. Papers
                    presented to the Economic History Society Conference* (Canterbury,
                    1983).

Palmer, C. J.   *The Perlustration of Great Yarmouth* 3 vols (Great Yarmouth, 1872–
                    5).
Parker, R. A. C.   *Coke of Norfolk: a financial and agricultural study, 1707–1842* (Oxford,
                    1975).
Phillips, H.   *The Thames about 1750* (1951).
Prothero, R. E.   *English Farming Past and Present* (1912; rev. ed. 1917).

Rose, R. B.   'Eighteenth-Century Price Riots and Public Policy in England',
                    International Review of Social History, VI (1961).

Samuel, R.   'British Marxist Historians, 1880–1980', Part One, *New Left Review*
                    120 (1980).
Saville, J.   'Primitive Accumulation and Early Industrialisation in Britain',
                    Socialist Register (1969).
Schama, S.   *Patriots and Liberators: revolution in the Netherlands, 1780–1813*
                    (1977).
Schove, D. J.   'The Preliminary Reduction of Wind and Pressure Observations in
                    N.W. Europe, A.D. 1648–1955' (University of London Ph.D.
                    thesis, 1958).

Schumpeter, E. B.   *English Overseas Trade Statistics, 1697–1808* with an Introduction by T. S. Ashton (Oxford, 1960).

Sen, S. R.   *The Economics of Sir James Steuart* (1957).

Slicher van Bath, B. H.   *The Agrarian History of Western Europe, 500–1850* (1963).

Smith, A.   *An Inquiry into the Nature and Causes of the Wealth of Nations* (1776; ed. J. R. McCulloch, 1838).

Smith, C.   *Three Tracts on the Corn Trade* (1766).

Steuart, J.   *An Inquiry into the Principles of Political Oeconomy* 2 vols (1767; ed. A. S. Skinner in two vols, Edinburgh and London, 1966).

Stout, W.   *The Autobiography of William Stout of Lancaster 1665–1752* (Manchester
ed. J. D. Marshall   Univ. Press, 1967).

Supple, B. E.   *Commercial Crisis and Change in England, 1600–1642* (Cambridge, 1959).

Sweezy, P.   'Communications – Comment on Brenner [The Origins of Capitalist Development: a critique of Neo-Smithian Marxism]', *New Left Review* 108 (1978).

Tawney, R. H.   *The Agrarian Problem in the Sixteenth Century* (1912).

Tawney, R. H. (ed.)   *Studies in Economic History: the collected papers of George Unwin* (1927).

Thirsk, J.   'Industries in the Countryside' in F. J. Fisher, (ed.) *Essays in the Economic and Social History of Tudor and Stuart England* (Cambridge, 1961).

Thirsk, J. (ed.)   *The Agrarian History of England and Wales*, vol. IV, *1500–1640* (1967).

Thirsk, J.   'Seventeenth-Century Agriculture and Social Change', in J. Thirsk (ed.), *Land, Church and People: essays presented to Prof. H. P. R. Finberg* (*Agricultural History Review Supplement*, 1970).

Thirsk, J. and   *Seventeenth Century Economic Documents* (Oxford, 1972).
Cooper, J. P.

Thompson, E. P.   'The Moral Economy of the English Crowd in the Eighteenth Century', *Past and Present* 50 (1971).

Thompson, E. P.   'The Peculiarities of the English', *Socialist Register* (1965), repr. in E. P. Thompson, *The Poverty of Theory and Other Essays* (1978).

Thornton, H.   *Historical Summary of the Corn Laws* (1841).

Tucker, J.   *A Brief Essay on the Advantages and Disadvantages which respectively attend France and Great Britain with regard to Trade* (1750).

Turner, M.   'Agricultural Productivity in England in the Eighteenth Century: evidence from crop yields', *Econ. Hist. Rev.,* 2nd ser. XXXV (1982).

Unger, W. S.   'Trade through the Sound in the Seventeenth and Eighteenth Centuries', *Econ. Hist. Rev.*, 2nd ser. XII (1960).

Unwin, G.   *Studies in Industrial Organisation in the Sixteenth and Seventeenth Centuries* (1904).

Uztariz, G. de   *The Theory and Practice of Commerce and Maritime Affairs*, trans. J. Kippax (1751).

Visser, C. *Verkeersindustrieen te Rotterdam in de tweede helft der Achttiende Eeuw* (Rotterdam, 1927).

Vries, Joh. de *De Economische Achteruitgang der Republiek in de Achttiende Eeuw* (Amsterdam, 1959).

Vries. J. de *The Dutch Rural Economy in the Golden Age, 1500–1700* (New Haven, 1974).

Voorthuijsen, W. D. *De Republiek der Verenigde Nederlanden en het Mercantilisme* ('S-Gravenhage, 1965).

Westerfield, R. B. *Middlemen in English Business, particularly between 1660 and 1760* (New Haven, 1915).

Willan, T. S. *The English Coasting Trade, 1600–1750* (Manchester, 1938).

Woude, A. M. van der 'Het Noorderkwartier. Een regional historisch onderzoek in de demografisch en economische geschiedenis van westelijk Nederland van de late middleeuwen tot het begin van de negentiende eeuw', *AAG Bijdragen* 16(1972) 3 vols.

Wrigley, E. A. 'A Simple Model of London's Importance in a Changing English Society and Economy, 1650–1750', *Past and Present* 37(1967).

Wrigley, E. A. and Schofield, R. S. *The Population History of England, 1541–1871: a reconstruction* (1981).

Wyczanski, A. 'Le Niveau de la Récolte des Céréales en Pologne du XVIe au XVIIIe Siècle', *Contributions and Communications, First International Economic History Conference, Stockholm* (Paris, 1960).

Young, A. *The Farmer's Letters to the People of England* (1767; 2nd ed. 1768).

Young, A. *The Expediency of a Free Exportation of Corn at this Time* (1770).

Youngson, A. J. *After the Forty-Five: the economic impact on the Scottish Highlands* (Edinburgh, 1973).

Index